Vegan 101

Cover photo © Getty Images.
Photos on the following pages from Shutterstock: 10, 15, 16, 17, 18, 22, 42, 60, 76, 94, 112, 132.
Photos on the following pages from Michael Maes: 13, 25, 33, 37, 49, 67, 75, 87, 99, 105, 121, 131, 137, 145.

Printed in China.

Library of Congress Cataloging-in-Publication Data

Vegan 101 : master vegan cooking with 101 great recipes / edited by Kate De-Vivo.

p. cm.

Includes index.

Summary: "A guide to vegan cooking including 101 recipes, equipment and pantry suggestions, how-to tips, glossary, and photographs"--Provided by publisher.

ISBN-13: 978-1-57284-122-2 (flexibound)

ISBN-10: 1-57284-122-2 (flexibound)

ISBN-13: 978-1-57284-686-9 (ebook)

ISBN-10: 1-57284-686-0 (ebook)

1. Vegan cooking. 2. Cookbooks. I. DeVivo, Kate. II. Title: Vegan one hundred one. III. Title: Vegan one hundred and one.

TX837.V39 2011

641.5'636--dc23

2011028663

10 9 8 7 6 5 4 3 2 1   15 14 13 12 11

Surrey Books is an imprint of Agate Publishing, Inc.

Agate and Surrey books are available in bulk at discount prices. For more information, go to agatepublishing.com.

Vegan 101

MASTER VEGAN COOKING WITH 101 GREAT RECIPES

EDITED BY **Kate DeVivo**

CONTENTS

INTRODUCTION

Agate Surrey Books is proud to introduce the 101 series, which aims to provide successful and fun cooking experiences for everyone from novices in the kitchen to more experienced cooks. *Vegan 101: Master Vegan Cooking with 101 Great Recipes* is one of the first books in this series, and it offers readers not only delicious recipes but also useful information about shopping for equipment, ingredients, kitchen essentials, and seasonings. Shopping for vegan fare can be intimidating, but we'll demystify the process for you. So whether you're considering following a strict vegan diet and don't know where to begin in preparing meals, or you're interested in trying some animal-free recipes in an effort to broaden your cooking skills as well as your palate, *Vegan 101* is a great place to start.

Most of the recipes in the 101 series books come from a wide range of Agate Surrey authors and editors. Contributors to *Vegan 101* include Sue Spitler, editor of the "1,001" series that includes titles like *1,001 Low-Fat Vegetarian Recipes* and *1,001 Best Slow-Cooker Recipes*; George Black and David Stowell, authors of *The Veganopolis Cookbook*; Kelly Rudnicki, author of *Vegan Baking Classics*; and Anupy Singla, author of *The Indian Slow Cooker*.

Vegan 101 recipes were selected to provide a starting point for anyone beginning their vegan-cooking journey. The collection includes a variety of cuisines (Italian, Mexican, Asian, and Indian, to name a few) and a range of cooking styles (baking, sautéing, roasting, slow cooking, and many more). Most of the recipes are basic, although a handful of them are more advanced; you'll find that all are easy to follow.

A TASTE OF WHAT YOU'LL FIND IN THIS BOOK

The Appetizers, Snacks, and Beverages chapter includes great dinner-party options, such as Black Bean Hummus, Pinto Avocado Dip, and Garbanzo Salsa, as well as delicious drinks like Hot Ginger Lemonade and Sangria. Hearty sandwiches like Portobello Mushroom Burgers with Caramelized Onions and Horseradish Cream Sauce and Meatless Sloppy Joes join other favorite recipes in the Sandwiches, Burgers, and Pizza chapter. While you're

flipping through that chapter, don't forget to try French-Style Onion Pizza or the Spanish Sandwich with Saffron Garlic Aioli. In the Pasta and Rice chapter, check out delicious dishes like Fusilli with Tomatoes and Corn; Fettuccine with Roasted Garlic, Onions, and Peppers; and Stir-Fried Rice Noodles with Vegetables.

Indian-Inspired Vegetable Soup, Curried Butternut Squash Soup (see photo on the previous page), and Mexican Tortilla Soup are just a few of the tasty offerings in the Soups and Stews chapter. Salads range from a simple Spinach and Melon Salad to German Potato Salad to Mango and Black Bean Salad and make a great addition to any vegan dish or can be served on their own. Bourbon Street Red Beans and Rice and Honey Glazed Roast Beets serve as terrific sides for many other Vegan 101 main-dish recipes. And the final chapter includes delicious desserts you won't want to miss, including Summer Blueberry Pie, Pumpkin Cookies, and Double Evil Brownies, just to name a few.

But before you get started cooking some of these great recipes, make sure you're up to speed on some vegan cooking basics, and that your kitchen and pantry are ready to go!

VEGAN COOKING BASICS

A vegan diet consists of food that is not made from any animal, animal product, or derivative. This means that vegan recipes exclude all meat, dairy, eggs, cheese, butter, and even honey. The vegan diet, and recipes in this book, is mostly based on fruits, vegetables, grains, beans, and legumes. It also often includes soy dairy alternatives, meat substitutes, and other vegan products. Cooking vegan fare, both at home and in restaurants, is one of the fastest-growing food trends in the United States.

KITCHEN EQUIPMENT BASICS

If you are just starting out with your own place or just learning to cook, you may not want to buy everything listed under Kitchen Equipment Basics. The items on the following list are the first that the beginner cook should purchase. Other equipment can be purchased as you need them over a period of a few years.

Appliances

We're sure you know this already, but your kitchen should include the following standard set of appliances.

Pretty Much Mandatory

- Refrigerator/freezers (set to about 34°F to 38°F, or as cold as you can get it without freezing vegetables or drinks)

- Freezer (if yours is not frost-free, you'll periodically need to unplug it to defrost your snow-filled box)

- Stove/oven (make sure the oven stays very clean, as burnt foods and other odors can affect the taste of your food)

- Microwave (again, make sure it's clean and ready for use)

- Blender (and not just for beverages and soups—you can use it in place of a food processor or an immersion blender in many instances)

- Hand mixer (well, you can always stir by hand, but sometimes, the hand mixer is indispensable)

Optional

- Food processor
- Immersion blender
- Stand mixer
- Slow cooker (4 to 6 quart; you will find several slow cooker recipes in this book)

Pots and Pans

The following are useful basic equipment for any kitchen.

- Skillets: Large 10-inch with lid and small 7- or 8-inch

- Saucepans: 1-quart and 3-quart with lids

- Baking pans: 13 × 9-inch and 9-inch square

- Baking sheets: Two that will fit in your oven with at least an inch of space on all sides

- Casserole: 2-quart Pyrex with lid

Optional

- Large stockpot with lid (8 quarts)
- 2 loaf pans (8 inches)
- Muffin pan (12 muffins)
- Pie pan (9 inches in diameter)

General Utensils

These are recommended basics for any kitchen.

- Knives: Chef's knife, serrated knife, and paring knife

- Measuring cups for both dry and liquid measures

- Measuring spoons

- Mixing bowls (two or three, ranging from 1 or 2 quarts to 5 or 6 quarts)

- Colander

- Cheese grater
- Citrus zester
- Salt and pepper mills
- Kitchen scissors
- Vegetable peeler
- Can opener
- Cooling rack
- Kitchen timer
- Cutting board
- Pot holders
- Kitchen towels

- Wooden spoons, slotted spoon, rubber or silicone spatula, ladle, whisk, tongs, and a large metal "flipper"

Storage and Cleaning

Either in a handy drawer or on a shelf, make sure you have all of these items within easy reach.

- Plastic or glass storage containers (5 to 10, varying sizes)
- Aluminum foil
- Plastic wrap
- Parchment paper
- Small baggies
- Large baggies
- Muffin pan liners

BASIC INGREDIENTS LIST FOR VEGAN COOKING

This section includes ingredients specific to vegan cooking, and you'll see them in the recipes in the book. There is no need to purchase all of these at once—buy herbs, spices, and ingredients as you need them and build your stock as you go.

Common Vegan Seasonings and Flavorings

- Basil
- Bay leaves
- Bouillon cubes (vegetable flavor)
- Cayenne pepper
- Chili powder
- Cumin
- Dry mustard
- Garlic powder
- Ground cinnamon
- Ground ginger
- Ground nutmeg
- Hot red pepper flakes
- Italian seasoning
- Oregano
- Paprika
- White pepper

Condiments and Ingredients

- Apple cider vinegar
- Balsamic vinegar
- Hot pepper sauce

- Ketchup
- Mustard
- Olive oil
- Red wine vinegar
- Rice vinegar
- Soy sauce
- Vegetable oil
- White wine vinegar

COMMON COOKING TERMS

You probably are quite familiar with most of these terms. If this is your first time cooking or it's been a while since you've been in the kitchen, here is a quick refresher:

- **Bake:** To cook food with dry heat, usually in the oven at a specified temperature.

- **Blanch:** A technique that involves immersing food in boiling water for a brief period of time and then immediately transferring into an ice bath in order to stop the cooking process. Blanching is an excellent technique for quickly cooking tender vegetables, as it helps them retain their firmness, crispness, and color.

- **Boil:** To cook food in boiling water (212°F) on the stovetop.

- **Broil:** To cook over a high heat at a specified distance from the heat source, usually in the oven or in the "broiler" part of the oven.

- **Deep fry:** To cook food by immersing it in preheated oil.

- **Grill:** To cook over an open flame on a metal framework, gridiron, or other cooking surface.

- **Roast:** To cook in an oven in an uncovered dish, usually resulting in a well-browned surface that seals in juices and flavors.

- **Sauté:** To cook food over a medium-high or high heat in a skillet or sauté pan in a small amount of oil, water, stock, or other liquid.

- **Steam:** To cook food with steam, usually in a steamer rack or basket positioned over (but not immersed in) a pan containing a small amount of water.

- **Stir-fry:** To cook over high heat with a small amount of oil; usually requires regular stirring as food is cooking. It can be used for several kinds of dishes and is often associated with Asian fare.

GENERAL COOKING TIPS

No matter what you're cooking or how many people you're serving, a few universal rules of the kitchen will make your life easier. The following is a list of our recommendations for the novice cook. These great habits will ensure fewer mistakes, less stress, and ultimately more delicious food.

- **Read every recipe from beginning to end, at least twice, before you start cooking.** This will help to ensure that you understand how it should be made and what you need to make it.

- **Set up your ingredients, pots, pans, and utensils before you begin to prepare the recipes.** We never start a recipe until we have every ingredient on the counter in front of us. (If possible, we also premeasure all the ingredients and have them ready to add, because there's nothing worse than accidentally dumping half a box of kosher salt into an almost-finished recipe.) If you know you'll need a greased pan in step 4, grease it and set it aside before you even get started.

- **Keep a grocery list and a pen attached to the refrigerator.** If you go to the grocery store without a specific list of what you need, you're likely to forget at least a few items.

- **Clean up as you go.** If you take the time to clean your dishes as you're cooking, you'll find that you will have more has more space to work in and less to do after the meal is done.

- **Time the meal.** It can be complicated to cook multiple recipes at once and make sure that everything ends up finishing at roughly the same time. Make sure you allow for enough time for everything to get done, and for recipes to be cooked simultaneously.

- **Be careful.** It sounds silly, but never forget that you're working with high-temperature appliances and cookware and sharp utensils! Use proper precaution when lifting lids, turning pans, and straining vegetables.

- **Have fun!** We hope you enjoy learning how to cook these vegan recipes and sharing them with others.

APPETIZERS, SNACKS, AND BEVERAGES

BERRY BREAKFAST SMOOTHIE

4 SERVINGS

INGREDIENTS

1 cup (236 mL) frozen strawberries
1 medium banana, sliced
1 cup (236 mL) vanilla soy yogurt
1 cup (236 mL) orange juice

1. Put all ingredients into blender, and purée until smooth. Serve in tall glasses.

SANGRIA >

6 SERVINGS (ABOUT 1 CUP [236 ML] EACH)

INGREDIENTS

4 cups (.95 L) dry red wine, chilled
2 cups (473 mL) orange juice, chilled
¼ cup (59 mL) lime juice
¾–1 cup (177–236 mL) sugar
½ each: thinly sliced lime, orange
Ice cubes

1. Mix all ingredients, except ice, in large pitcher; pour over ice cubes in tall glasses.

HOT GINGER LEMONADE

12 SERVINGS (ABOUT ½ CUP [118 ML] EACH)

INGREDIENTS

5 cups (1.2 L) water
¾ cup (177 mL) each: lemon juice, sugar
2-inch (5 cm) piece gingerroot, sliced

1. Combine all ingredients in slow cooker; cover and cook on high 2 to 3 hours (if mixture begins to boil, turn heat to low); turn to low to keep warm for serving.

VARIATION

Hot Cranberry Mint Lemonade—Make recipe as above, substituting 2½ (591 mL) cups cranberry juice for 2½ (591 mL) cups of the water; omitting gingerroot. Add 1 tablespoon (15 mL) dried mint leaves, tied in cheesecloth bag, during last 1 hour of cooking.

HOT CURRIED PARTY MIX

10 SERVINGS (ABOUT ½ CUP [118 ML] EACH)

INGREDIENTS

3 cups (708 mL) rice cereal squares
1 cup (236 mL) sesame sticks
½ cup (118 mL) each: cashews, roasted peanuts, wasabi
   peas
2 tablespoons (30 mL) vegan margarine, melted
1½ (7.5 mL) teaspoons each: soy sauce, curry powder,
   sugar

1. Heat slow cooker on high 15 minutes; add cereal, sesame sticks, nuts, and wasabi peas.

2. Drizzle mixture with combined margarine and soy sauce and toss; sprinkle with combined curry powder and sugar and toss.

3. Cook, uncovered, on high 1½ hours, stirring every 30 minutes. Turn slow cooker to low to keep warm for serving or remove from slow cooker and cool.

BLACK BEAN HUMMUS

This recipe comes from 1,001 Low-Fat Vegetarian Recipes *by Sue Spitler.*

6 SERVINGS (ABOUT ¼ CUP EACH)

INGREDIENTS

1 can (15 ounces [425 mL]) black beans, rinsed, drained
¼ cup (59 mL) reduced-sodium vegetable broth or water
2–3 tablespoons (30–45 mL) tahini
3 cloves garlic
2–2½ tablespoons (30–37.5 mL) lemon juice
1½ tablespoons (22.5 mL) soy sauce
Salt and cayenne pepper, to taste
Pita Chips (recipe follows) or pita breads, cut into wedges

1. Process beans, broth, tahini, garlic, lemon juice, and soy sauce in food processor until smooth; season to taste with salt and cayenne pepper. Refrigerate 1 to 2 hours for flavors to blend. Serve with Pita Chips.

PITA CHIPS

6 SERVINGS (8 EACH)

INGREDIENTS

3 whole wheat pocket breads
Vegetable oil cooking spray
3–4 teaspoons (15–20 mL) dried Italian seasoning or other desired herbs

1. Open breads and separate each into 2 halves; cut each half into 8 wedges. Arrange wedges, soft sides up, in single layer on jelly-roll pan. Spray with cooking spray and sprinkle with Italian seasoning. Bake at 425°F (220°C) until browned and crisp, 5 to 10 minutes.

VARIATION

Seasoned Pita Chips—Make recipe above, substituting 1 to 2 teaspoons (15–30 mL) chili powder, ground cumin, or garlic powder for the Italian seasoning.

EGGPLANT MARMALADE

12 SERVINGS (ABOUT 3 TABLESPOONS [45 ML] EACH)

INGREDIENTS

2 medium eggplants (1¼ pounds [566 gm] each), unpeeled, cubed
⅓ cup (79 mL) coarsely chopped onion
2 tablespoons (30 mL) minced roasted garlic
3 tablespoons (45 mL) each: minced gingerroot, light brown sugar
1½ teaspoons (7.5 mL) fennel seeds, crushed
2 tablespoons (30 mL) red wine vinegar
2 teaspoons (10 mL) Asian sesame oil
⅓ cup (79 mL) golden raisins
⅓ cup (79 mL) reduced-sodium vegetable broth
2–3 tablespoons (30–45 mL) toasted pine nuts or slivered almonds
Whole wheat lavosh, or crackers, for serving

1. Combine eggplant, onion, garlic, gingerroot, brown sugar, and fennel seeds; toss with vinegar and oil and arrange in single layer on greased, foil-lined jelly-roll pan. Bake at 425°F (220°C) until eggplant is browned and wrinkled, about 1½ hours, stirring every 30 minutes.

2. Stir raisins and broth into mixture; bake until broth is absorbed, 10 to 15 minutes. Stir in pine nuts and cool. Refrigerate overnight for flavors to blend. Serve with lavosh.

ZUCCHINI BREAD

2 LOAVES, 32 SERVINGS

INGREDIENTS

4 tablespoons (59 mL) water

½ cup (118 mL) each: vegetable oil, unsweetened apple-sauce

2 cups (473 mL) sugar

1 teaspoon (5 mL) vanilla extract

2 cups (473 mL) grated, unpeeled zucchini

4 cups (.95 L) unbleached all-purpose flour

3½ teaspoons (17.5 mL) ground cinnamon

2 teaspoons (10 mL) baking soda

1½ teaspoons (7.5 mL) baking powder

1 teaspoon (5 mL) salt

1. Preheat oven to 350°F (180°C), and spray two 8 × 4-inch [21.25 × 11.25-cm] loaf pans with vegetable oil baking spray.

2. In bowl of stand mixer fitted with paddle attachment, beat the water, vegetable oil, applesauce, sugar, and vanilla on low speed until blended. Stir in zucchini and mix well.

3. Combine flour, cinnamon, baking soda, baking powder, and salt in bowl with wire whisk. Stir dry ingredients into zucchini mixture until just combined. Pour into prepared pans, and bake 50 to 60 minutes, or until inserted cake tester comes out clean.

4. Cool completely before slicing.

GARLIC BREAD

Select a good quality vegan loaf for this aromatic bread, or use sour-dough bread for a flavorful variation.

4 SERVINGS

INGREDIENTS

4 thick slices vegan bread (multi-grain, stone ground whole wheat, potato, sourdough)
Olive oil cooking spray
2 cloves garlic, cut into halves

1. Spray both sides of bread generously with cooking spray. Broil on cookie sheet 4 inches from heat source until browned, about 1 minute on each side.

2. Rub both sides of hot toast with cut sides of garlic.

PINTO BEAN AND AVOCADO DIP >

12 SERVINGS (ABOUT 2 TABLESPOONS [30 ML] EACH)

INGREDIENTS

1 can (15 ounces [425 gm]) pinto beans, rinsed, drained
¾ cup (177 mL) finely chopped onion
2 cloves garlic, minced
½ jalapeño pepper, minced
3 tablespoons (45 mL) finely chopped cilantro
1 large tomato, chopped
½ medium avocado, chopped
Salt and pepper, to taste
Baked tortilla chips

1. Process beans in food processor or blender until smooth; add onion, garlic, jalapeño pepper, and cilantro and process until blended. Mix in tomato and avocado; season to taste with salt and pepper. Refrigerate 1 to 2 hours for flavors to blend. Serve with tortilla chips.

GARBANZO SALSA

8 SERVINGS (ABOUT $\frac{1}{3}$ CUP [79 ML] EACH)

INGREDIENTS

1 can (15½ ounces [439 gm]) garbanzo beans, rinsed, drained
¾ cup (177 mL) each: chopped, seeded cucumber, quartered cherry tomatoes
3 green onions with tops, thinly sliced
¼ cup (59 mL) chopped yellow bell pepper
2 tablespoons (30 mL) each: finely chopped mint, cilantro
2–3 cloves minced garlic
2–3 teaspoons (10–15 mL) olive oil
Lemon juice, to taste

1. Combine all ingredients, except lemon juice, in bowl and toss; season to taste with lemon juice.

FRIED RIPE PLANTAINS

If you purchase green plantains, they will ripen more quickly if kept in a closed paper bag.

4 SERVINGS

INGREDIENTS

Canola, or peanut, oil
2 ripe plantains, peeled, diagonally cut into ¼-inch slices
Salt, to taste

1. Heat 1½ to 2 inches (3.5 to 5 cm) of oil to 375°F (190°C) in large saucepan. Fry plantains until golden on both sides; drain well on paper toweling. Season to taste with salt and serve hot.

VARIATION

Sweet Plantains—Make recipe as above, omitting salt. Sprinkle plantains with sugar-cinnamon mixture.

ROASTED GARLIC AND HERB CANNELLINI DIP

A good-for-you dip that tastes terrific! Italian cannellini beans are white kidney beans that are similar in flavor and appearance to navy or Great Northern beans.

6 SERVINGS (ABOUT ¼ CUP [59 ML] EACH)

INGREDIENTS

1 can (15 ounces [425 gm]) cannellini or Great Northern beans, rinsed, drained
1 teaspoon (5 mL) minced roasted garlic
1 tablespoon (15 mL) each: olive oil, prepared horseradish
2 tablespoons (30 mL) minced chives
½ teaspoon (2.5 mL) each: dried oregano and basil leaves
2–3 drops hot pepper sauce
2–3 teaspoons (10–15 mL) lemon juice
Salt and white pepper, to taste
Dippers: Pita Chips (page 28) and assorted vegetables

1. Process beans, garlic, olive oil, and horseradish in food processor until smooth. Mix in chives, oregano, basil, and hot pepper sauce. Season to taste with lemon juice, salt, and white pepper. Refrigerate 1 to 2 hours for flavors to blend. Serve with dippers.

SESAME WONTON CUPS >

8 SERVINGS (2 EACH)

INGREDIENTS

24 wonton wrappers (vegan or eggless)
2 teaspoons (10 mL) Asian sesame oil
1 cup (236 mL) thinly sliced napa cabbage
½ cup (118 mL) each: broccoli sprouts, thinly sliced snow
   peas, shredded carrots
1 green onion, thinly sliced
Sweet Sesame Dressing (recipe follows)
Wasabi peas and toasted hemp or sesame seeds, for garnish

1. Lightly brush edges of wonton wrappers with Asian sesame oil.
   Press wontons, oil side up, in miniature muffin cups to form
   shells, using every other cup in muffin pan so that edges do
   not touch. Bake at 350°F (180°C) until lightly browned, 6 to 7
   minutes. Cool on wire racks.

2. Combine cabbage, sprouts, snow peas, carrots, and green onion in bowl; pour Sweet Sesame Dressing over and toss. Spoon
   mixture into wonton cups and garnish each with 2 or 3 wasabi
   peas and a sprinkling of hemp seeds.

SWEET SESAME DRESSING

MAKES ABOUT ½ CUP (118 ML)

INGREDIENTS

1 tablespoon Asian sesame oil
2–3 tablespoons (30–45 mL) rice wine vinegar
⅓ cup (79 mL) apricot preserves
1 teaspoon (5 mL) each: soy sauce, minced gingerroot
2–3 (10–15 mL) teaspoons peanut butter

1. Mix all ingredients.

CURRIED ONION BAKLAVA

8 SERVINGS

INGREDIENTS

2 pounds onions, thinly sliced
3 tablespoons (45 mL) curry powder
¼ cup (59 mL) all-purpose flour
½ cup (118 mL) orange juice
¼ cup (59 mL) each: chopped mango chutney,
   dried apricots
Salt and pepper, to taste
¼ cup (59 mL) ground almonds
½ cup (118 mL) ground ginger snaps
½ teaspoon (2.5 mL) ground cinnamon
Vegetable oil cooking spray
10 sheets frozen vegan phyllo, thawed
½ cup (118 mL) water
3 tablespoons (45 mL) each: sugar and maple syrup

1. Sauté onions in lightly greased large skillet 5 minutes; cook, covered, over medium-low heat until onions are very tender, 15 to 20 minutes. Sprinkle with curry powder and flour and cook, stirring, 1 minute. Stir in orange juice, chutney, and apricots; heat to boiling. Reduce heat and simmer, uncovered, until apricots are softened and mixture thickened, about 5 minutes. Season to taste with salt and pepper; cool.

2. Combine almonds, ginger snaps, and cinnamon. Spray bottom of 13 × 9-inch (33 × 23-cm) baking pan with cooking spray. Fold 1 sheet of phyllo in half crosswise and place in pan; spray with cooking spray and sprinkle with 4 teaspoons (20 mL) almond mixture. Repeat with phyllo and almond mixture four times, ending with phyllo.

3. Spread onion mixture over phyllo. Add remaining phyllo and almond mixture in layers, as in step 2, ending with phyllo. Spray phyllo with cooking spray and score with sharp knife into serving pieces. Bake at 350°F (180°C) for 45 minutes, covering loosely with foil if becoming too brown. Cut into pieces while hot.

4. Heat water, sugar, and maple syrup to boiling in small saucepan, stirring to dissolve sugar. Pour mixture over hot baklava. Cool 10 to 15 minutes before serving, or cool completely and serve at room temperature.

SWEET ONION TARTE TATIN

For best flavor, use a sweet onion, such as Vidalia.

6–8 SERVINGS

INGREDIENTS

1 tablespoon sugar
2½ pounds (1.2 kg) small sweet onions, halved crosswise
Salt and pepper
⅓ cup (79 mL) dark or light raisins
1 teaspoon (5 mL) dried thyme leaves
¼ teaspoon (1.25 mL) ground allspice
1½ cups (354 mL) reduced-sodium vegetable broth
2 teaspoons (10 mL) balsamic vinegar
Tarte Tatin Crust (recipe follows)

1. Heat lightly greased 12-inch (30 cm) skillet with ovenproof handle over medium heat until hot; sprinkle bottom evenly with sugar. Place onion halves, cut sides down, in skillet, fitting in as many as possible. Cut remaining onion halves into pieces, or chop coarsely, and fill in any spaces between onion halves. Sprinkle lightly with salt and pepper; sprinkle with raisins, thyme, and allspice. Cook, uncovered, over medium heat until onions begin to brown on the bottoms, 8 to 10 minutes.

2. Add broth and vinegar to skillet; heat to boiling. Reduce heat and simmer, covered, until onions are tender, 20 to 25 minutes. Heat to boiling; reduce heat and simmer rapidly, uncovered, until liquid is almost gone.

3. Roll pastry for Tarte Tatin Crust on floured surface into 13-inch (33 cm) circle. Ease pastry over onions in skillet, tucking in edges to fit. Bake at 375°F (190°C) until pastry is browned and juices are bubbly, 30 to 35 minutes. Cool in pan on wire rack 10 minutes; place large serving plate over skillet and invert onto plate. Serve warm or at room temperature.

TARTE TATIN CRUST

1½ cups (354 mL) all-purpose flour
½ teaspoon (2.5 mL) baking powder
½ teaspoon (2.5 mL) dried thyme leaves
Pinch salt
4 tablespoons (59 mL) cold vegan margarine, cut into
   pieces
5–6 tablespoons (75–90 mL) ice water

1. Combine flour, baking powder, thyme, and salt in medium
   bowl; cut in margarine until mixture resembles coarse crumbs.
   Add water 1 tablespoon at a time, mixing lightly with fork after
   each addition, until dough just holds together. Form dough
   into disk. Refrigerate, covered, at least 30 minutes.

SANDWICHES, BURGERS, AND PIZZA

GYROS SANDWICH

INGREDIENTS

2 tablespoons (30 mL) each: dried oregano leaves, black
  pepper
1 tablespoon (15 mL) each: ground cumin, paprika
1 teaspoon (5 mL) each: ground cinnamon, garlic powder
½ teaspoon (2.5 mL) cayenne pepper
2 pounds (1 kg) seitan, cut into strips (1-inch [2.5-cm])
1 red onion, cut into six wedges
8 cloves garlic,
1 cup (236 mL) red wine vinegar
Juice of 1 lemon
Cucumber Sauce (recipe follows)
6–8 sandwich-sized pita pockets
4 cups (.95 L) chopped romaine lettuce
2 cucumbers, sliced
2 large tomatoes, sliced

1. Combine oregano, black pepper, cumin, paprika, cinnamon, garlic powder, and cayenne pepper. Rub seitan strips with spice mixture. Place seitan strips, onion, and garlic, in medium roasting pan or 13 × 9-inch (33 × 23-cm) baking pan.

2. Pour combined vinegar and lemon juice over all, mixing well. Cover and let stand 2 hours at room temperature, or refrigerate overnight.

3. Preheat oven to 400°F (200°C). Cover pan tightly with foil and roast about 1 hour. Remove foil.

4. Grill seitan strips and onions on well-oiled hot grill or griddle, or sauté over medium-high heat in large skillet.

5. Warm pita bread. Spread some of Cucumber Sauce inside pita breads. Fill pita breads with seitan strips, onion, lettuce, and cucumber and tomato slices. Serve with remaining Cucumber Sauce.

CUCUMBER SAUCE

INGREDIENTS

1 cup (236 mL) plain soy yogurt
¼ cup (50 mL) peeled, seeded, and diced cucumber
1 teaspoon (5 mL) dill weed
2 tablespoons (30 mL) fresh lime or lemon juice
½ teaspoon (2.5 mL) each: salt, paprika

1. Mix all ingredients and chill.

PEANUTTY AND JELLY SANDWICHES

You won't believe the rich peanut butter flavor of this creamy, low-fat sandwich spread. It's great on raisin bread or crackers, topped with sliced banana or apple.

6 SERVINGS

INGREDIENTS

¾ cup (177 mL) drained canned Great Northern beans
⅓ cup (79 mL) reduced-fat smooth, or chunky, peanut butter
2 tablespoons (30 mL) halved raisins
1–2 tablespoons (15–30 mL) maple syrup
12 slices whole wheat, or multigrain, bread
¾ cup (177 mL) grape, or other flavor, jam

1. Process beans in food processor until smooth; mix in peanut butter, raisins, and maple syrup. Spread on 6 slices bread; top with jam and remaining bread slices.

MEDITERRANEAN SANDWICH

This is a light and delicious summertime sandwich. It is loosely based on the popular sandwich known in Nice as pan bagnat. *The essential ingredient is a large crusty roll, which is stuffed with fresh spinach and the Mediterranean mixture. Serve alone or with a side of roasted potatoes, sliced tomatoes or fruit.*

12 SERVINGS

INGREDIENTS

2 cups (473 mL) Cashew Ricotta (recipe follows)
1 cup (236 mL) vegan pesto
1 cup (236 mL) Roasted Artichoke Hearts (recipe follows)
½ cup (118 mL) sun-dried tomatoes in oil, julienned
½ cup (118 mL) pitted Kalamata olives, halved
12 ciabatta rolls, approximately 8 inches (20 cm) in diameter and 3 inches (7.5 cm) high, or similar large, crusty rolls
3 cups (708 mL) spinach leaves

1. Combine the Cashew Ricotta, pesto, Roasted Artichoke Hearts, sun-dried tomatoes, and olives in a large bowl, mixing well.

2. Cut a ½-inch-thick (1-cm-thick) slice off top of each roll. Scoop out inside of each roll, leaving a shell about 1 inch thick (2.5 cm); warm rolls on grill. Stuff each roll with layer of fresh spinach and then artichoke mixture. Replace tops of the rolls and diagonally slice each sandwich in half.

CASHEW RICOTTA

4 SERVINGS (1 CUP [95 ML] EACH)

INGREDIENTS

4 cups (.95 L) raw, unsalted cashews
1 or more cups (236 mL or more) fermented wheat berry
 water
Juice of 1 lemon
Salt, to taste

1. Soak the cashews in water for 4 to 6 hours. Drain and rinse them well in cold running water.

2. Process the cashews in a food processor, adding just enough of the fermented wheat berry water to produce a thick, ricotta-like mixture.

3. Season the mixture with the lemon juice and enough salt to bring out the flavors nicely. And there you have it—ricotta without the cow.

ROASTED ARTICHOKE HEARTS

INGREDIENTS

1 (14-ounce [397-gm]) can artichoke hearts, drained
¼ cup (59 mL) olive oil
1 teaspoon (5 mL) each: salt, pepper

1. Preheat oven to 400°F (200°C). Line baking sheet with parchment paper.

2. Combine all ingredients, tossing to coat. Arrange on prepared baking sheet and roast 15 minutes, or until edges just begin to brown.

PORTOBELLO MUSHROOM BURGERS WITH CARAMELIZED ONIONS AND HORSERADISH CREAM SAUCE >

Large portobello mushrooms work beautifully as a substitute for beef patties. They are dressed up here with caramelized onions and horseradish sauce. If you don't like horseradish, ketchup, mustard, or vegan mayonnaise are also great choices.

4 SERVINGS

INGREDIENTS

4 large portobello mushrooms
4 tablespoons (60 mL) olive oil, divided
Salt and pepper
3 tablespoons (45 mL) balsamic vinegar, divided
2 onions, very thinly sliced
Crusty rolls or burger buns
Horseradish Cream Sauce (recipe follows)
Chopped romaine lettuce
Tomato slices

1. Preheat the oven to 400°F (200°C). Line baking sheet with parchment paper.

2. Remove stems from mushrooms, and, using sharp paring knife, carefully cut away dark gills from underside of each mushroom. Make a few shallow slashes in top surface of each mushroom.

3. Lightly oil mushrooms with 2 tablespoons (30 mL) olive oil and season them generously with salt and pepper. Arrange them on prepared baking sheet and drizzle the mushrooms with 2 tablespoons of the vinegar. Roast 15 to 18 minutes, or until mushrooms begin to soften and darken a bit. Remove from oven and set aside.

4. Heat remaining 2 tablespoons oil in large skillet over very low heat. Add onions; cook, stirring occasionally, for 20 to 40 minutes, until onions are golden brown. Season to taste with salt, pepper, and remaining 1 tablespoon vinegar. Remove from heat and set aside.

5. Grill rolls or buns and mushrooms on medium-hot grill or in large, lightly oiled skillet. Spread the Horseradish Cream Sauce on insides of the rolls. Place lettuce on bottoms of rolls. Top with each with mushroom, onion slices and tomato slices.

HORSERADISH CREAM SAUCE

INGREDIENTS

1 cup (236 mL) vegan mayonnaise
2 tablespoons (30 mL) prepared horseradish or grated
   fresh horseradish
Salt, to taste (optional)

1. Mix mayonnaise and horseradish. Season to taste with salt, if desired.

SLOPPY JOES

8–10 SERVINGS

INGREDIENTS
¼ cup (60 mL) canola oil
1 each: red onion, red and green bell pepper, diced
2 teaspoons (10 mL) black pepper
1 tablespoon (15 mL) each: paprika, dark chili powder
2 teaspoons (10 mL) garlic powder
1 (6-ounce [168-gm]) can tomato paste
6–8 vegan burgers, crumbled
1 cup (236 mL) root beer or cola
Salt, to taste
8–10 crusty rolls or burger buns
Fresh spinach leaves (optional)
Thinly sliced red onion (optional)

1. Heat oil in large skillet over medium-high heat. Add onion, bell peppers, black pepper, paprika, chili powder, and garlic powder. Sauté until onion and peppers are soft and mixture is fragrant. Stir in tomato paste.

2. Add crumbled burger in small handfuls, and cook until burger is browned, stirring frequently. Stir in root beer. Cook until hot. Season to taste with salt.

3. Layer roll bottoms with spinach leaves, if desired. Top with Sloppy Joes mixture and onion slices, if desired

SPANISH SANDWICH WITH SAFFRON GARLIC AIOLI

Here's a sandwich that's fancy enough to serve at a brunch or dinner party and would pair well with a nice Spanish white wine. This recipe comes from The Veganopolis Cookbook *by David Stowell and George Black.*

4 SERVINGS

INGREDIENTS

6 tablespoons (90 mL) extra virgin olive oil
10 cloves garlic, finely minced
2 large tomatoes, diced
4 tablespoons (59 mL) Italian parsley, finely chopped
2 tablespoons (30 mL) seasoned rice vinegar
Pepper, to taste
1 cup (236 mL) vegetable stock
1 pound (454 gm) seitan, cut into bite-sized pieces
½ cup (118 mL) dry white wine
Generous pinch saffron
1 cup (236 mL) vegan mayonnaise
4 ciabatta rolls or similar large, crusty rolls
Spinach leaves
1 cup (236 mL) roasted red peppers, sliced lengthwise into strips
1 cup (236 mL) pitted Kalamata olives, halved

1. Preheat oven to 350°F (180°C). Line roasting pan with parchment paper.

2. Heat olive oil in skillet over medium-low heat. Add 2 tablespoons (30 mL) garlic. Sauté for a few seconds, then add tomatoes and parsley and cook until tomatoes start to break up.

3. Add the seasoned rice vinegar and a generous grinding of black pepper. Allow the mixture to cook down for a few minutes, and then add the stock.

4. Bring the mixture to a boil and cook until it is reduced by half. Reserve 3 tablespoons (45 mL) of the mixture in a separate cup or small bowl and cool it down in the refrigerator or freezer.

5. Place the seitan pieces in the prepared roasting pan and pour the contents of the sauté pan over it. Mix well with your hands. Cover the pan tightly with aluminum foil and bake for about 30 minutes.

6. While the seitan is roasting, prepare the saffron aioli. Heat the white wine in a small saucepan over high heat. Add the saffron and allow it to cook down to just a few tablespoons (15 to 30 mL) of bright orange-colored liquid. Add 1 tablespoon (15 mL) of the minced garlic and the cooled reserved tomato-parsley mixture. Stir it well again before using it.

7. Stir in the mayonnaise. Store the aioli in the refrigerator and stir it well again before using it.

8. To assemble the sandwiches, cut each roll in half and lightly grill them. Cover each bottom half with spinach leaves and place about ¼ pound (112 gm) of the seitan mixture on top of that. Garnish with a few strips of the saffron aioli on the inside of the top half of each roll and replace the top on each sandwich. Diagonally slice each sandwich in half and serve.

FALAFEL BURGERS WITH TAHINI DRESSING

4 SERVINGS

INGREDIENTS

1½ cups (354 mL) cooked dried or drained, canned
   garbanzo beans, coarsely pureed
¼ cup (59 mL) finely chopped parsley
2 tablespoons (30 mL) chopped onion
2 cloves garlic, minced
1–2 tablespoons (15–30 mL) lemon juice
¼ cup (59 mL) all-purpose flour
1¼ teaspoons (6.25 mL) ground cumin
Salt and pepper, to taste
2 pita breads, halved
Tahini Dressing (recipe follows)
¼ cup (59 mL) each: chopped tomato, cucumber, thinly
   sliced green onions

1. Mix garbanzo beans, parsley, onion, garlic, lemon juice, flour, and cumin in bowl; season to taste with salt and pepper.

2. Shape mixture into 4 burgers and cook in lightly greased skillet until browned, 3 to 4 minutes on each side. Arrange burgers in pitas; drizzle 2 tablespoons (30 mL) Tahini Dressing over each burger. Spoon combined tomato, cucumber, and sliced green onions into pitas.

TAHINI DRESSING

INGREDIENTS

⅓ cup (79 mL) fat-free vegan yogurt
2–3 tablespoons (30–45 mL) tahini (sesame seed paste)
1 small clove garlic, minced
½–1 teaspoon (2.5–5 mL) lemon juice

1. Mix all ingredients; refrigerate until ready to use.

VARIATION

Falafel Pitas—Make recipe as above, but shape mixture into meatballs; coat lightly with unseasoned dry bread crumbs. Spray meatballs with vegetable oil cooking spray and bake at 375°F (190°C) until browned, about 15 minutes. Serve in pitas.

FRENCH-STYLE ONION PIZZA

6 SLICES

INGREDIENTS

6 cups (1.4 L) thinly sliced onions
2 medium tomatoes, coarsely chopped
¼ cup (59 mL) finely chopped parsley
½ teaspoon (2.5 mL) each: dried oregano and thyme
   leaves
Salt and pepper, to taste
Basic Pizza Dough
2–4 tablespoons (30–60 mL) sliced black olives

1. Cook onions in lightly greased large skillet over medium to medium-low heat until very tender, about 15 minutes. Add tomatoes, parsley, oregano, and thyme; cook over medium heat until mixture is thick, about 15 minutes. Season to taste with salt and pepper; cool.

2. Shape dough on greased 12-inch (30-cm) pizza pan, making rim around edge. Spread onion mixture over dough and sprinkle with olives. Bake at 425°F (220°C) until crust is browned, 15 to 20 minutes.

BASIC PIZZA DOUGH

MAKES ONE 12-INCH (30-CM) CRUST (6 LARGE SLICES)

    1¼ cups (315 mL) all-purpose flour, divided
    1 package quick-rising yeast
    ½ teaspoon (2.5 mL) sugar
    ¼ teaspoon (1.25 mL) salt
    ½ cup (118 mL) very hot water (120°F [49°C])

1. Combine ¾ cup (177 mL) flour, yeast, sugar, and salt in bowl; add hot water, stirring until smooth. Mix in enough remaining ½ cup (118 mL) flour to make a soft dough. Knead on floured surface until smooth and elastic, 3 to 5 minutes. Cover dough with bowl and let stand 15 minutes.

CANNELLINI BEAN PATTIES WITH FRESH TOMATO RELISH

4 SERVINGS

INGREDIENTS

1 can (15 ounces [425 gm]) cannellini beans, or other white
   beans, rinsed, drained, coarsely pureed
½ cup (118 mL) finely chopped tomato
¼ cup (59 mL) each: finely chopped onion, green bell pepper
1½ teaspoons (7.5 mL) minced garlic
2–4 tablespoons (30–60 mL) yellow cornmeal
1–1½ teaspoons (7.5 mL) Italian seasoning
Salt and pepper, to taste
4 slices Italian bread or 4 whole-wheat buns, toasted
1 clove garlic, cut in half
Fresh Tomato Relish (recipe follows)

1. Combine beans, tomato, onion, bell pepper, garlic, cornmeal, and Italian seasoning; season to taste with salt and pepper.

2. Shape mixture into 4 patties; cook in lightly greased large skillet over medium heat until browned, about 5 minutes on each side. Rub tops of bread slices with cut sides of garlic; top with patties and serve with Fresh Tomato Relish.

FRESH TOMATO RELISH

MAKES ABOUT 1 CUP (236 ML)

INGREDIENTS

1 cup (236 mL) chopped tomato
1 tablespoon (15 mL) finely chopped fresh, or 1 teaspoon
   dried basil leaves
1 tablespoon (15 mL) each: olive oil, red wine vinegar
Salt and pepper, to taste

1. Mix tomato, basil, oil, and vinegar; season to taste with salt and pepper.

VEGGIE-TOFU BURGERS

Healthy vegetables, tofu, and crunchy walnuts combine in these sweetened burgers.

4 SERVINGS

INGREDIENTS

⅔ cup (160 mL) each: finely chopped onion, shredded carrots
2 teaspoons (10 mL) minced roasted garlic
2 cups (473 mL) firmly packed chopped spinach
1 package (10½ ounces [298 gm]) light tofu, well drained, crumbled
2 sun-dried tomatoes (not in oil), softened, chopped
2 tablespoons (30 mL) reduced-sodium tamari soy sauce
1 tablespoon (15 mL) maple syrup
½ cup (118 mL) coarsely chopped walnuts
¾ cup (177 ml) unseasoned dry bread crumbs, divided
Salt and pepper, to taste
4 whole wheat buns, toasted
Spicy brown mustard, or vegan mayonnaise

1. Sauté onion, carrots, and garlic in lightly greased large skillet 2 to 3 minutes. Add spinach, tofu, sun-dried tomatoes, soy sauce, and maple syrup to skillet. Cook, covered, over medium heat until vegetables are tender, about 5 minutes. Cook, uncovered, until mixture is dry, about 5 minutes, stirring occasionally. Process in food processor until finely chopped; stir in walnuts and ½ cup (118 mL) bread crumbs; season to taste with salt and pepper.

2. Shape mixture into 4 burgers and coat with remaining ¼ cup (59 mL) bread crumbs; cook in lightly greased skillet until browned, about 5 minutes on each side. Serve in buns with mustard.

PASTA

CURRIED PASTA AND VEGETABLES

This delicate curry dish is garnished with chopped peanuts and mango chutney for a wonderful flavor and texture contrast.

4 ENTRÉE SERVINGS

INGREDIENTS

½ cup (118 mL) each: chopped red and yellow bell pepper
1 cup (236 mL) each: small cauliflower florets, peas or cut green beans
½ teaspoon (2.5 mL) red pepper flakes
¼ cup (59 mL) water
Salt and pepper, to taste
2 cups (473 mL) Curry Sauce (recipe follows)
8 ounces (224 gm) angel hair pasta, cooked, warm
2–4 tablespoons (30–60 mL) chopped dry-roasted peanuts
¼ cup (59 mL) packed cilantro, chopped
¼ cup (59 mL) chopped mango chutney

1. Sauté bell peppers in lightly greased medium skillet until tender, 3 to 4 minutes. Add cauliflower, peas, red pepper flakes, and water; heat to boiling. Reduce heat and simmer, covered, until vegetables are tender, 5 to 8 minutes; cook, uncovered, until water has evaporated; season to taste with salt and pepper. Toss with Curry Sauce and pasta; sprinkle with peanuts and cilantro. Serve chutney on the side.

CURRY SAUCE

4 SERVINGS (ABOUT ½ CUP EACH)

INGREDIENTS

¼ cup finely chopped onion
4 cloves garlic, minced
2 tablespoons flour
2 teaspoons curry powder
¼ teaspoon cayenne pepper
2 cups reduced-sodium vegetable broth
1 tablespoon cornstarch
¼ cup dry white wine, or water
Salt and pepper, to taste

1. Sauté onion and garlic in lightly greased medium saucepan 2 to 3 minutes; stir in flour, curry powder, and cayenne pepper. Cook 1 minute, stirring. Add broth and heat to boiling. Stir in combined cornstarch and wine; boil, stirring, until thickened, about 1 minute. Season to taste with salt and pepper.

FETTUCCINE WITH ROASTED GARLIC, ONIONS, AND PEPPERS

Deceptively simple to make, and incredibly delicious to eat!

8 SIDE-DISH SERVINGS

INGREDIENTS

2 bulbs garlic
Olive oil cooking spray
3 medium onions, cut into wedges
2 large red bell peppers, cut into ½-inch (1-cm) slices
2 tablespoons (30 mL) each: olive oil, lemon juice, chopped
   parsley
½ teaspoon (2.5 mL) salt
¼ teaspoon (1.25 mL) pepper
8 ounces (224 gm) fettuccine, cooked, warm

1. Cut a scant ½ inch (1 cm) off tops of garlic bulbs, exposing ends of cloves; spray with cooking spray. Wrap garlic bulbs loosely in foil. Arrange garlic, onions, and bell peppers in single layer on greased foil-lined jelly-roll pan. Roast at 425°F (220°C) until garlic is very soft and vegetables are tender, 30 to 40 minutes.

2. Cool garlic slightly; squeeze pulp into small bowl. Stir in oil, lemon juice, parsley, salt, and pepper. Toss with pasta and onion mixture.

PASTA WITH GREENS, RAISINS, AND PINE NUTS

Radicchio, escarole, curly endive, kale, or mustard greens can be substituted for the brightly colored oriental kale in this sweet-and-bitter Italian favorite.

4 ENTRÉE SERVINGS

INGREDIENTS

4 each: sliced medium onions, minced cloves garlic
1 tablespoon (15 mL) olive oil
1 teaspoon (5 mL) sugar
12 ounces (340 gm) oriental kale leaves, torn
⅓ cup (79 mL) dark raisins
½ cup (118 mL) reduced-sodium vegetable broth
Salt and pepper, to taste
8 ounces (224 gm) whole wheat spaghetti, or linguine, cooked, warm
2 tablespoons (30 mL) pine nuts, or slivered almonds

1. Sauté onions and garlic in oil in large skillet until tender, 3 to 5 minutes. Stir in sugar; cook over low heat until onions are golden, 10 to 15 minutes, stirring occasionally. Stir in kale, raisins, and broth; cook, covered, over low heat until kale is wilted, about 10 minutes. Season to taste with salt and pepper. Toss with spaghetti; sprinkle with pine nuts.

Note: For a shorter prep time, begin cooking the pasta before preparing the rest of the recipe.

PASTA SANTA FE >

Flavors of the Southwest merge with pasta; this one is picante, with poblano chilies.

4 ENTRÉE SERVINGS

INGREDIENTS

1 medium onion, sliced

3 cloves garlic, minced

2 tablespoons (30 mL) canola oil

2 each: sliced medium zucchini, poblano peppers, sliced tomatoes

1 cup (236 mL) whole-kernel corn

2 tablespoons (30 mL) chili powder

1 teaspoon (5 mL) dried oregano leaves

½ teaspoon (2.5 mL) ground cumin

2 tablespoons (30 mL) chopped cilantro

Salt and pepper, to taste

8 ounces (224 gm) trio maliano (combination of corkscrews, shells, and rigatoni) pasta, cooked, warm

1. Sauté onion and garlic in oil in large skillet until tender, about 5 minutes. Add zucchini, poblano peppers, tomatoes, corn, chili powder, oregano, and cumin. Cook, uncovered, over medium heat until vegetables are crisp-tender, about 10 minutes. Stir in cilantro; season to taste with salt, and pepper. Toss with pasta.

Note: For a shorter prep time, begin cooking the pasta before preparing the rest of the recipe.

RIGATONI WITH VEGETARIAN SAUSAGE AND FENNEL PESTO

The aromatic flavor of fennel makes this dish very special!

6 ENTRÉE SERVINGS

INGREDIENTS

1 package (12¾ ounces [361 gm]) vegan Italian-style
    sausages, crumbled
1½ cups (354 mL) thinly sliced fennel bulb, or celery
1 cup (236 mL) chopped onion
2 cloves garlic, minced
1 can (8 ounces [224 gm]) reduced-sodium whole toma-
    toes, drained, chopped
Fennel Pesto (recipe follows)
12 ounces (340 gm) rigatoni, or other tube pasta, cooked,
    warm

1. Sauté vegan sausage, fennel, onion, and garlic in lightly greased medium skillet until onion is tender, 5 to 8 minutes. Stir in tomatoes and Fennel Pesto. Heat to boiling; reduce heat and simmer, covered, until fennel is tender, about 15 minutes. Toss with pasta.

FENNEL PESTO

6 SERVINGS (SCANT ¼ CUP EACH)

INGREDIENTS

1 tablespoon (15 mL) fennel seeds
1 cup (236 mL) chopped fennel bulb, or celery
½ cup (118 mL) loosely packed parsley
2 cloves garlic
3 tablespoons (45 mL) water
1 tablespoon (15 mL) olive oil
¼ cup (1 ounce [28 gm]) each: grated vegan Parmesan
  cheese, walnuts
Salt and pepper, to taste

1. Soak fennel seeds in hot water in small bowl; let stand 10 minutes; drain. Process fennel seeds and remaining ingredients, except salt and pepper, in food processor or blender until almost smooth. Season to taste with salt and pepper. Serve at room temperature.

Note: This pesto can also be served with sliced tomatoes. Or, stir some into vegan sour cream for a marvelous veggie dip.

SESAME PASTA SALAD WITH SUMMER VEGETABLES

6 SIDE-DISH SERVINGS

INGREDIENTS

1 small eggplant
1 cup (236 mL) each: sliced carrots, sliced yellow summer
    squash, broccoli florets, cooked until crisp-tender
1 medium red bell pepper, sliced
¼ cup (59 mL) sliced green onions
8 ounces (224 gm) thin spaghetti, cooked, room
    temperature
Sesame Dressing (recipe follows)
2 teaspoons (10 mL) toasted sesame seeds

1. Pierce eggplant 6 to 8 times with fork; place in greased baking pan. Roast, uncovered, until tender, for 30 minutes; cool. Cut eggplant in half; scoop out pulp and cut into ¾-inch (2-cm) pieces, discarding skin. Combine eggplant pieces, carrots, squash, broccoli, bell pepper, green onions, and spaghetti in large bowl; toss with Sesame Dressing and sprinkle with sesame seeds.

SESAME DRESSING

MAKES ABOUT ⅓ CUP (79 ML)

INGREDIENTS

2 tablespoons (30 mL) each: reduced-sodium soy sauce,
    Asian sesame oil
1 teaspoon (5 mL) hot chili oil (optional)
1 tablespoon (15 mL) balsamic, or red wine, vinegar
1½ tablespoons (22.5 mL) sugar
1 clove garlic, minced
1 tablespoon (15 mL) chopped cilantro, or parsley

1. Mix all ingredients.

ZITI WITH GREMOLATA

The fresh lemon flavor of the Gremolata accents this tomato and pasta dish. Serve with Garlic Bread (see p. 31) and a robust red wine.

8 ENTRÉE SERVINGS

INGREDIENTS

½ cup (118 mL) chopped onion
8 ounces (224 gm) shiitake, or cremini, mushrooms, sliced
2 cans (14½ ounces [411 gm] each) diced tomatoes with
   Italian seasoning, undrained
Salt and pepper, to taste
1 pound (454 gm) ziti, or penne, cooked, warm
Gremolata (recipe follows)

1. Sauté onion and mushrooms in lightly greased large skillet until tender, 5 to 8 minutes. Add tomatoes with liquid and heat to boiling; reduce heat and simmer, uncovered, until thickened, about 10 minutes. Season to taste with salt and pepper. Toss with pasta and ½ the Gremolata; serve with remaining Gremolata.

GREMOLATA

INGREDIENTS

4 servings (about 2 tablespoons each)
1 cup (236 mL) packed parsley
1–2 teaspoons (5–10 mL) grated lemon zest
4 large cloves garlic
Salt, to taste

1. Process all ingredients, except salt, in food processor until minced; season to taste with salt. Stir into sauces and soups as desired.

Note: This pungent seasoning mixture can also be added to soups, pastas, or rice dishes for a flavor accent.

SOUTHWEST PASTA WITH CILANTRO PESTO

If poblano peppers are not available, substitute green bell peppers and add 1 to 2 teaspoons minced jalapeño pepper to the onions when sautéing.

6 ENTRÉE SERVINGS

INGREDIENTS

3 cups (708 mL) each: peeled, cubed acorn squash, sliced
   zucchini
1 medium onion, sliced
3 poblano peppers, sliced
1–1½ teaspoons (5–7.5 mL) dried oregano leaves
¼–½ teaspoon (1.25–2.5 mL) ground cumin
1 tablespoon (15 mL) olive oil
¾ cup (177 mL) reduced-sodium vegetable broth
2 medium tomatoes, cut into wedges
Salt and pepper, to taste
12 ounces (340 gm) fettuccine, or other flat pasta, cooked,
   warm
Cilantro Pesto (recipe follows)

1. Sauté acorn squash, zucchini, onion, poblano peppers, oregano, and cumin in oil in large skillet 3 minutes; add broth and heat to boiling. Reduce heat and simmer, covered, until acorn squash is crisp-tender, about 5 minutes. Add tomatoes; cook, covered, until softened, 3 to 4 minutes. Season to taste with salt and pepper. Toss fettuccine with Cilantro Pesto; top with vegetables.

Note: For a shorter prep time, begin cooking the fettuccine before preparing the rest of the recipe.

CILANTRO PESTO

6 SERVINGS (ABOUT 2 TABLESPOONS EACH)

INGREDIENTS

1½ cups (354 mL) packed cilantro leaves
½ cup (118 mL) packed parsley
1 clove garlic
¼ cup (1 ounce [28 gm]) grated vegan Parmesan cheese
3 tablespoons (45 mL) pine nuts, or walnuts
1 tablespoon (15 mL) each: olive oil, lemon juice
Salt and pepper, to taste

1. Process all ingredients, except salt and pepper, in food processor or blender until almost smooth. Season to taste with salt and pepper. Serve at room temperature.

STIR-FRIED RICE NOODLES WITH VEGETABLES >

Rice noodles are also called cellophane noodles, or "bihon." The dried noodles are soaked in cold water to soften, then drained before using.

4 ENTRÉE SERVINGS (ABOUT 1½ CUPS EACH)

INGREDIENTS

1 package (8 ounces [224 gm]) rice noodles
1 cup (236 mL) each: cut green beans, cubed yellow summer squash
½ cup (118 mL) each: thinly sliced celery, red bell pepper
4 green onions, thinly sliced
1 tablespoon finely chopped fresh gingerroot
1 tablespoon (15 mL) canola oil
2 cups (473 mL) shredded napa cabbage
1 cup (236 mL) reduced-sodium vegetable broth
2 tablespoons (30 mL) dry sherry (optional)
2–3 teaspoons (10–15 mL) light soy sauce
½–1 teaspoon (2.5–5 mL) Szechuan chili sauce

1. Place noodles in large bowl; cover with cold water. Let stand until noodles separate and are soft, about 15 minutes; drain.

2. Stir-fry green beans, squash, celery, bell pepper, green onions, and gingerroot in oil in large wok or skillet until tender, 8 to 10 minutes. Add cabbage and stir-fry 1 minute. Stir in noodles and remaining ingredients. Heat to boiling; reduce heat and simmer, uncovered, until noodles have absorbed all liquid, about 5 minutes.

SOUPS
AND STEWS

BEAN GAZPACHO

Pureed beans contribute nutritional value, plus a velvety texture, to this delicious gazpacho.

6 SERVINGS (ABOUT 1½ CUPS [354 ML] EACH)

INGREDIENTS

2 cans (15½ ounces [440 gm] each) pinto beans, rinsed, drained
1 quart (3.8 L) reduced-sodium tomato juice
3–4 tablespoons (45–60 mL) lime juice
2 teaspoons (10 mL) chopped garlic
1 cup (236 mL) each: thick and chunky salsa, peeled, seeded, chopped cucumber, sliced celery
½ cup (118 mL) each: sliced green onions, chopped green bell pepper
½ small avocado, peeled, chopped
½ cup (118 mL) vegan sour cream
¾ cup (177 mL) Herb Croutons (recipe follows)

1. Process beans, tomato juice, lime juice, and garlic in food processor or blender until smooth; pour into large bowl. Mix in remaining ingredients, except avocado, sour cream, and Herb Croutons. Refrigerate until chilled, 3 to 4 hours.

2. Mix avocado into soup; garnish each bowl of soup with a dollop of sour cream and sprinkle with croutons.

HERB CROUTONS

12 SERVINGS (¼ CUP [59 ML] EACH)

INGREDIENTS

3 cups (708 mL) cubed firm, or day-old, French, or Italian, bread (½–¾ inch)
2 teaspoons (10 mL) dried herbs or herb combinations
Vegetable oil cooking spray

1. Spray bread cubes with vegetable oil cooking spray; sprinkle with 2 teaspoons (10 mL) dried herbs and toss. Arrange in single layer on jelly-roll pan. Bake at 375°F (190°C) until browned, 8 to 10 minutes, stirring occasionally. Cool; store in airtight container up to 2 weeks.

SPLIT PEA SOUP

A perfect entree soup for hearty appetites on a crisp autumn or winter day. Serve with thick slices of Garlic Bread (see p. 31).

6 ENTRÉE SERVINGS

INGREDIENTS

1½ cups (354 mL) chopped onions
1 cup (236 mL) chopped carrots
½ cup (118 mL) sliced celery
1 tablespoon (15 mL) canola oil
6 cups (1.4 L) water
1¾ cups (413 mL) vegetable stock
1 pound (454 gm) dried split peas, rinsed, sorted
1 teaspoon (5 mL) dried marjoram leaves
Salt and pepper, to taste

1. Sauté onions, carrots, and celery in oil in large saucepan until tender, 8 to 10 minutes. Add water, stock, split peas, and marjoram; heat to boiling. Reduce heat and simmer, covered, until peas are tender, 1 to 1¼ hours. Season to taste with salt and pepper.

BLACK BEAN AND OKRA GUMBO

The gumbo is delicious served over warm cornbread.

8 ENTRÉE SERVINGS

INGREDIENTS

1 pound (454 gm) smoked vegan turkey sausage, sliced
1 can (14½ ounces [411 gm]) stewed tomatoes with chilies
2 cans (15 ounces [425 gm] each) black beans, rinsed, drained
1 cup (236 mL) vegetable broth
2 cups (473 mL) small mushrooms
1 cup (236 mL) each: chopped onion, red and green bell peppers, sliced carrots
1 tablespoon (15 mL) chili powder
1 teaspoon (5 mL) gumbo file
2 cups (473 mL) frozen cut okra, thawed
Salt and pepper, to taste

1. Combine all ingredients, except okra, salt, and pepper, in 6-quart slow cooker; cover and cook on low 6 to 8 hours, adding okra during last 30 minutes. Season to taste with salt and pepper

INDIAN-INSPIRED VEGETABLE SOUP

This recipe is a great example of blending fresh vegetables with Indian lentils and spices. You may substitute any vegetables you have on hand, such as cauliflower, spinach, or broccoli. You can also try using barley or wild rice as the grain, and substituting another lentil for the moong dal.

8 ENTRÉE SERVINGS

INGREDIENTS

2 yellow or white onions, chopped
2 large tomatoes, chopped
1 (2-inch [5 cm]) piece gingerroot, minced or grated
3 cloves garlic, chopped or grated
4 large carrots, chopped
4 stalks celery, chopped
½ head green cabbage, chopped
2 tablespoons (30 mL) each: dried whole moong dal with skin, brown rice, quinoa
1 tablespoon (15 mL) cumin seeds
½ teaspoon (2.5 mL) ground turmeric
Salt and pepper, to taste
Shredded vegan cheese (any kind), for garnish
Crushed tortilla chips, for garnish

1. Combine all ingredients in slow cooker. Cover by 2 inches with water; cover and cook on high 7 hours. Using an immersion blender, partially blend soup, or process 3 cups of the soup in a blender, and return it to the slow cooker. Season to taste with salt and pepper. Garnish with a little cheese and tortilla chips.

Note: To make this dish in a 3½-quart slow cooker, halve all the ingredients and proceed with the recipe. A half recipe makes 7 cups (1.66 L).

SPICED BEAN CHILI WITH FUSILLI

Use your favorite beans and any shaped pasta in this versatile chili.

8 ENTRÉE SERVINGS

INGREDIENTS

1 pound (454 gm) lean ground vegan meat substitute
2 cans (14½ ounces [411 gm] each) diced tomatoes with roasted garlic, undrained
1 can (15 ounces [425 gm]) each: garbanzo and dark red kidney beans, rinsed, drained
2 cups (473 mL) chopped onions
1 cup (236 mL) sliced cremini or white mushrooms
½ cup (118 mL) each: sliced celery, dry white wine or water
2 tablespoons (30 mL) chili powder
¾ teaspoon (3.75 mL) each: dried oregano and thyme leaves, ground cumin
8 ounces (224 gm) fusilli, cooked
Salt and pepper, to taste
3–4 tablespoons (45–60 mL) sliced green or black olives

1. Cook meat substitute in lightly greased large skillet over medium heat until browned, 8 to 10 minutes, crumbling with a fork. Combine meat substitute and remaining ingredients, except fusilli, salt, pepper, and olives, in 6-quart slow cooker; cover and cook on low 6 to 8 hours, adding pasta during last 20 minutes. Season to taste with salt and pepper; sprinkle each bowl of soup with olives.

VIETNAMESE CURRIED COCONUT SOUP

Rice stick noodles, made with rice flour, can be round or flat. They must be softened in water before using. Cooked angel hair pasta can be substituted.

6 FIRST-COURSE SERVINGS (ABOUT 1 CUP [236 ML] EACH)

INGREDIENTS

1 tablespoon minced garlic
3–4 tablespoons (45–60 mL) curry powder
3½ cups (828 mL) vegetable stock
3 cups (708 mL) reduced-fat coconut milk
2 tablespoons (30 mL) minced gingerroot
½ cup (118 mL) each: sliced green onions, yellow onion
2 tablespoons (30 mL) minced parsley
1 tablespoon (15 mL) grated lime zest
½–1 teaspoon (2.5–5 mL) oriental chili paste
¼ cup (59 mL) each: lime juice, chopped cilantro
Salt and white pepper, to taste
8 ounces (224 gm) rice stick noodles

1. Sauté garlic in lightly greased large saucepan 1 minute; stir in curry powder and cook, stirring, 30 seconds. Add stock, coconut milk, gingerroot, onions, parsley, lime zest, and chili paste; heat to boiling. Reduce heat and simmer, covered, 15 minutes. Stir in lime juice and cilantro; season to taste with salt and white pepper.

2. Prepare noodles according to package directions. Spoon noodles into soup bowls; ladle soup over noodles.

TUSCAN BEAN SOUP

This recipe comes from 1,001 Low-Fat Vegetarian Recipes *by Sue Spitler.*

8 ENTRÉE SERVINGS (ABOUT 1½ CUPS [681 ML] EACH)

INGREDIENTS

1 cup (236 mL) chopped onion
½ cup (118 mL) each: chopped celery, green bell pepper
2 teaspoons (10 mL) minced roasted garlic
2 tablespoons (30 mL) olive oil
1 tablespoon (15 mL) all-purpose flour
1½ teaspoons (7.5 mL) dried Italian seasoning
2 bay leaves
7 cups (1.7 L) reduced-sodium vegetable broth
2 cans (15 ounces [425 gm] each) cannellini, or Great Northern, beans, rinsed, drained
2 tablespoons (30 mL) reduced-sodium tomato paste
½ cup (118 mL) quick-cooking barley
1 large Idaho potato, unpeeled, cut into ½-inch (1-cm) pieces
1 cup (236 mL) sliced carrots
1 cup (236 mL) packed baby spinach leaves
Salt and pepper, to taste

1. Sauté onion, celery, bell pepper, and garlic in oil in Dutch oven until tender, about 5 minutes. Stir in flour, Italian seasoning, and bay leaves; cook 1 minute longer. Add broth, beans, and tomato paste and heat to boiling; reduce heat and simmer, uncovered, 20 to 25 minutes, adding barley, potato, carrots, and spinach during last 10 minutes of cooking time. Discard bay leaves. Season to taste with salt and pepper.

CURRIED BUTTERNUT SQUASH SOUP

Acorn or hubbard squash can also be used in this fragrant soup. See photo on page 13.

8 FIRST-COURSE SERVINGS (ABOUT 1 CUP [236 ML] EACH)

INGREDIENTS

½ cup (118 mL) chopped onion
1 clove garlic, mashed
2 teaspoons (10 mL) olive oil
4 cups (.95 L) reduced-sodium vegetable broth
2 pounds (.91 kg) butternut squash, peeled, seeded, cubed
2 medium tomatoes, chopped
1½ teaspoons (7.5 mL) curry powder
1 cup (236 mL) coarsely chopped cilantro leaves and stems
Salt and pepper, to taste
Chopped cilantro, for garnish

1. Sauté onion and garlic in oil in large saucepan until tender, about 5 minutes. Add broth, squash, tomatoes, and curry powder and heat to boiling; reduce heat and simmer, covered, until squash is tender, about 10 minutes. Process soup and cilantro in blender or food processor until smooth; season to taste with salt and pepper. Serve warm; garnish each bowl of soup with cilantro sprigs.

VARIATION

Savory Herbed Squash Soup—Make recipe above, omitting tomatoes, curry powder and cilantro; add ¾ teaspoon (3.75 mL) each dried thyme and marjoram leaves and ¼–½ teaspoon (1.25–2.5 mL) ground mace.

ITALIAN VEGAN MEATBALL STEW >

Italian-style vegan sausage links, cut into 1-inch pieces, can be substituted for the meatballs.

8 ENTRÉE SERVINGS (ABOUT 1½ CUPS [354 ML] EACH)

INGREDIENTS

1 each: medium chopped onion, sliced red, or green, bell pepper
2 cans (14½ ounces [411 gm] each) tomatoes with roasted garlic, undrained
1 cup (236 mL) reduced-sodium vegetable broth
1 can (15 ounces [425 gm]) cannellini, or Great Northern, beans, rinsed, drained
4 medium potatoes, unpeeled, cubed
8 ounces (224 gm) broccoli rabe, coarsely chopped
2 medium carrots, sliced
2 tablespoons (30 mL) balsamic vinegar
1 teaspoon (5 mL) each: dried oregano and basil leaves
1 package (12 ounces [340 gm]) vegan meatballs, warm
½ cup (118 mL) frozen peas
Salt and pepper, to taste
Grated vegan parmesan cheese, for garnish

1. Sauté onion and bell pepper in lightly greased large saucepan until tender, about 5 minutes. Add tomatoes, broth, beans, potatoes, broccoli rabe, carrots, vinegar, oregano and basil; heat to boiling. Reduce heat and simmer, covered, until vegetables are tender, about 20 minutes.

2. Stir in meatballs and peas; cook until hot, about 5 minutes. Season to taste with salt and pepper; garnish each serving with cheese.

CREAM OF BROCCOLI SOUP

8 SERVINGS (1½ CUPS [354 ML] EACH)

INGREDIENTS

2 quarts (1.9 L) rice or soy milk
2 or 3 heads fresh broccoli, cut into florets
¼ cup (59 mL) olive oil
⅓ cup (79 mL) white spelt flour
3 shallots, very finely diced
Zest and juice of 1 lemon
2 teaspoons (10 mL) white pepper
½ teaspoon (2.5 mL) each: grated nutmeg, cayenne pepper
Salt and black pepper, to taste

1. Fill large pot with water and heat to boiling. Salt the boiling water generously. Add the broccoli and cook about 8 minutes. Drain and cool under cold running water.

2. Meanwhile, heat rice milk in large saucepan over medium heat until hot; keep warm.

3. In large soup pot or Dutch oven, heat oil over medium-high heat. Whisk in flour, whisking until mixture just starts to darken, about 4 minutes. Whisk in the shallots, lemon zest, white pepper, nutmeg, and cayenne pepper. Season to taste with salt. Cook 2 minutes.

4. Add hot rice milk, 2 cups (473 mL) at a time, whisking between each addition until creamy. Add most of the broccoli, reserving 10 or 15 of the smallest ones to use for garnish.

5. Simmer about 15 minutes. Using an immersion blender, blend until smooth, or blend it in batches in food processor; return to pot and heat. Add reserved florets. Stir in lemon juice and season to taste with black pepper.

VARIATION

Cream of Broccoli and Corn Soup—Make recipe above, adding 2 cups (473 mL) fresh or frozen corn kernels after blending the soup mixture. Cook 10 minutes over medium heat, stirring frequently.

SAVORY MUSHROOM AND BARLEY SOUP

Using quick-cooking barley speeds preparation. Other grains, such as wild rice or oat groats, can be substituted for the barley; cook according to package directions and add to soup during the last 30 minutes of cooking time.

4 ENTRÉE SERVINGS

INGREDIENTS

3 cups water
1 can (14½ ounces [411 gm]) diced tomatoes, undrained
¾ cup (177 mL) each: chopped onion, celery, carrots
1 teaspoon (5 mL) dried savory leaves
¾ teaspoon (7.5 mL) crushed fennel seeds
2 cups (473 mL) sliced cremini or white mushrooms
½ cup (118 mL) quick-cooking barley
Salt and pepper, to taste

1. Combine all ingredients, except barley, salt, and pepper, in slow cooker; cook on high 4 to 6 hours, adding barley during last 30 minutes. Season to taste with salt and pepper.

VARIATIONS

Savory Mushroom and Spinach Soup—Make recipe above, adding 2 to 3 cloves sliced garlic. Omit barley; add 3 cups (708 mL) torn spinach during last 15 minutes of cooking time.

Maple Bean and Mushroom Soup—Make recipe above, adding 2 cloves minced garlic, 1 to 2 tablespoons (15–30 mL) maple syrup, and 1 can (15 ounces [425 gm]) drained Great Northern beans; omit barley.

ASIAN MUSHROOM SOUP WITH NOODLES

Two kinds of mushrooms contribute rich flavor to this soup.

6 ENTRÉE SERVINGS (ABOUT 1½ CUPS [354 ML] EACH)

INGREDIENTS

2 pounds (.91 kg) cremini mushrooms, sliced, divided
½ cup (118 mL) minced onion
1 clove garlic, minced
½ teaspoon (2.5 mL) dried thyme leaves
2 tablespoons (30 mL) canola oil
1½ quarts (1.4 L) vegetable broth
½ cup (118 mL) dry white wine, or vegetable broth
1 ounce (28 gm) dried shiitake mushrooms
4 ounces (112 gm) uncooked low-carb whole wheat
   linguini or soba noodles
1 cup (236 mL) snow peas
⅓ cup (79 mL) thinly sliced radishes
1 tablespoon (15 mL) red wine vinegar
Salt and pepper, to taste

1. Sauté half the cremini mushrooms, onion, garlic, and thyme in oil in large saucepan until soft, 5 to 8 minutes. Add broth, wine, and shiitake mushrooms; heat to boiling. Reduce heat and simmer, covered, 30 minutes.

2. Strain soup, discarding mushrooms; return broth to saucepan. Add remaining ingredients, except salt and pepper; simmer, uncovered, until pasta is al dente, about 8 minutes. Season to taste with salt and pepper.

THREE-ONION SOUP
WITH MUSHROOMS

For a soup with a richer flavor, sprinkle onions, leeks, and shallots with 1 teaspoon sugar and cook in 1 tablespoon vegan margarine in large skillet over medium low heat until onions are golden, about 15 minutes.

6 FIRST-COURSE SERVINGS

INGREDIENTS
6½ cups (1.5 L) vegetable broth
3 cups (708 mL) thinly sliced onions
1½ cups (354 mL) thinly sliced leeks
½ cup (118 mL) chopped shallots or green onions
2 cups (473 mL) sliced mushrooms
1 teaspoon (5 mL) sugar
Salt and pepper, to taste

1. Combine all ingredients, except salt and pepper, in 6-quart slow cooker; cover and cook on low 6 to 8 hours. Season to taste with salt and pepper.

TOFU AND VEGETABLE STEW

As with most stews, the vegetables in this dish can be varied depending on the season and availability; tempeh can be substituted for the tofu.

4 ENTRÉE SERVINGS (ABOUT 1¾ CUPS [315 ML] EACH)

INGREDIENTS
½ cup (118 mL) each: sliced onion, celery
3 cloves garlic, minced
4 cups (.95 L) reduced-sodium vegetable broth
2 cups (473 mL) each: sliced carrots, unpeeled, cubed red potatoes (½-inch [.5-cm])
1 bay leaf
1 teaspoon (5 mL) ground cumin
½ teaspoon (2.5 mL) dried thyme leaves
½ package (10-ounce [284 gm] size) baby spinach
1 package (10½ ounces [298 gm]) firm light tofu, cubed (½-inch [.5-cm])
Salt and pepper, to taste

1. Sauté onion, celery, and garlic in lightly greased large saucepan until softened, about 4 minutes. Add broth, carrots, potatoes, bay leaf, cumin, and thyme; heat to boiling. Reduce heat and simmer, covered, until vegetables are tender, about 15 minutes.

2. Add spinach and tofu and simmer 3 to 4 minutes. Discard bay leaf; season to taste with salt and pepper.

MEXICAN TORTILLA SOUP

10 SERVINGS (ABOUT 1½ CUPS [354 ML] EACH)

INGREDIENTS

3 quarts (2.9 L) vegetable stock

3 tablespoons (45 mL) olive or canola oil

2 white onions, finely diced

6 cloves garlic, crushed

1 (8-ounce [224-g]) can diced Hatch or other mild green chili peppers (optional)

2 jalapeño peppers, seeded and finely diced

2 teaspoons (10 mL) each: ground cumin, dried oregano leaves, dark chili powder

4 carrots, peeled and diced

1 cup (236 mL) finely shredded green cabbage

2 cups (473 mL) chopped seitan

1 (12-ounce [340-g]) can diced tomatoes, undrained

Fresh lime juice, to taste

Hot pepper sauce, to taste

Salt, to taste

8 fresh corn tortillas, cut into wedges and fried crisp, or about 32 packaged corn tortilla chips (unsalted preferred)

Fresh cilantro leaves, for garnish

1. Heat the vegetable stock in Dutch oven over medium heat.

2. Meanwhile, in large soup pot, heat oil over medium-high heat. Add onions, garlic, green chili peppers peppers, jalapeño pepper, cumin, oregano, and chili powder, and cook until onions are softened. Stir in carrots, cabbage, seitan, and tomatoes.

3. Add hot stock and heat to boiling; simmer over low heat until carrots are tender, about 30 minutes. Season to taste with lime juice, hot pepper sauce, and salt.

4. Break up tortilla chips and place some in bottom of each soup bowl. Ladle hot soup over chips and garnish with cilantro leaves.

SALADS

GRILLED TOFU SALAD WITH AVOCADO

This salad has a pleasant combination of temperature, texture, and color that you will love.

1 SERVING

INGREDIENTS

⅓ pound (150 g) extra-firm tofu
Generous handful mesclun lettuce mix
2 tablespoons (30 mL) seasoned rice vinegar
1 fresh avocado, peeled, pitted, quartered, and sliced lengthwise
1 fresh tomato, sliced
1 cucumber, stripe peeled and sliced
Finely chopped parsley, for garnish

1. Preheat grill or broiler.

2. Grill tofu on each side until it is lightly browned. Slice it lengthwise in half and grill the newly cut sides. Remove it from the grill and slice it into triangles.

3. Dress lettuce with rice vinegar, or dressing of your choice, and mound it in center of chilled plate. Arrange sliced avocado, tomato and cucumber on one side of plate. Top the salad with tofu triangles.

4. Garnish with parsley and serve.

BLUE PEAR WALNUT SALAD

This salad depends on a vegan blue cheese substitute for its flavor. The only one currently on the market is offered by a Scottish manufacturer called Isle of Butte and marketed under the name Scheese. Black Duck Imports distributes it in the United States. Ask your grocer if it can be made available in your local store. You may also find Chicago Soy-dairy's Teese Vegan Mozzarella to be a wonderful substitute.

2 SERVINGS

INGREDIENTS

3 ounces (85 g) spinach leaves or mesclun mix
½ cup (118 mL) vinaigrette dressing
1 ripe Bartlett, Anjou, or red pear, cored, quartered, and
    thinly sliced into 4 'fans'
1 cucumber, stripe peeled and sliced
½ cup (118 mL) toasted walnuts, chopped
2 ounces (56 g) vegan blue cheese substitute, finely diced
Pepper, to taste

1. To assemble salads, toss spinach in bowl with vinaigrette dressing, and transfer to centers of 2 chilled plates.

2. Arrange 2 thinly sliced pear fans at side of each plate. Cover rest of plate with sliced cucumbers. Mound walnuts in center of salad, and sprinkle vegan blue cheese over all.

3. Season to taste with pepper and serve.

MANGO AND BLACK BEAN SALAD >

Any tropical fruit, such as kiwi, papaya, or star fruit, can be used in this refreshing salad.

4 ENTRÉE SERVINGS (ABOUT 1 CUP EACH)

INGREDIENTS

4 large ripe mangoes, peeled, pitted, cubed
1 cup (236 mL) cubed pineapple
½ medium cucumber, seeded, sliced
¼ cup (59 mL) finely chopped red bell pepper
4 small green onions, thinly sliced
1 can (15 ounces [425 gm]) black beans, rinsed, drained
Salad Dressing (recipe follows)
Mint sprigs, for garnish

1. Combine all ingredients, except mint, and toss. Garnish with mint.

SALAD DRESSING

MAKES ABOUT ⅓ CUP (79 ML)

INGREDIENTS

2 tablespoons (30 mL) each: olive oil, water
1 tablespoon (15 mL) each: maple syrup, tarragon wine vinegar, grated lime zest
3–4 teaspoons (15–20 mL) lime juice
½ teaspoon (2.5 mL) dried mint leaves
Pinch salt

1. Mix all ingredients.

ORANGE-MARINATED BEAN SALAD

This medley of beans is enhanced with a fresh accent of orange.

6 ENTRÉE SERVINGS (ABOUT ⅔ CUP [158 ML] EACH)

INGREDIENTS

1 can (15 ounces [425 mL]) each: adzuki and red kidney beans, rinsed, drained
1 cup (236 mL) thinly sliced cabbage
⅓ cup (79 mL) each: thinly sliced green onions, yellow bell pepper, celery, carrot
Orange Dressing (recipe follows)
Salt and white pepper, to taste
3 large red bell peppers, halved
Shredded lettuce, for garnish

1. Combine beans, cabbage, green onions, sliced bell pepper, celery, and carrot; pour Orange Dressing over and toss; season to taste with salt and white pepper. Spoon salad into bell pepper halves; serve on lettuce-lined plates.

ORANGE DRESSING

MAKES ABOUT ½ CUP (118 ML)

INGREDIENTS

⅓ cup (79 mL) orange juice
¼ cup (59 mL) white wine vinegar
2 tablespoons (30 mL) olive oil
2 cloves garlic, minced
1 tablespoon (15 mL) finely chopped cilantro
2 teaspoons (10 mL) grated orange zest

1. Mix all ingredients.

CABBAGE, CARROT, AND PARSLEY SLAW

Make this slaw early in the day. The raw, organic apple cider gives the slaw a bright flavor and promotes digestion.

10 SERVINGS (½ CUP [118 ML] EACH)

INGREDIENTS

2 cups (473 mL) each: shredded red and green cabbage

4 large carrots, peeled and finely julienned or shredded in a food processor

1 cup (236 mL) Italian parsley, finely chopped

¼ cup (59 mL) raw, organic apple cider vinegar

½ cup (118 mL) seasoned rice vinegar

2 tablespoons (30 mL) liquid amino acids (available from many grocers)

2 tablespoons (30 mL) turbinado sugar

1. Combine all the ingredients in large bowl and mix well. Cover and refrigerate several hours. Serve alongside sandwiches, soups, or entrées.

CHILI-DRESSED SALAD WITH RADIATORE

A fun pasta, radiatore look like the tiny radiators for which they are named! Other shaped pastas can be used, if preferred.

4 ENTRÉE SERVINGS (ABOUT 1½ CUPS [354 ML] EACH)

INGREDIENTS

3 cups (708 mL) radiatore, cooked
1½ cups (354 mL) broccoli florets
2 medium tomatoes, cut into wedges
½ cup (118 mL) cooked whole-kernel corn
½ medium avocado, cubed (¾-inch [2-cm])
2 tablespoons (30 mL) finely chopped cilantro
Chili Dressing (recipe follows)

1. Combine all ingredients and toss.

CHILI DRESSING

MAKES ABOUT ¼ CUP (59 ML)

INGREDIENTS

3 tablespoons (45 mL) lemon juice
2 tablespoons (30 mL) olive oil
½ teaspoon (2.5 mL) chili powder
¼ teaspoon (1.25 mL) salt
¼ teaspoon (1.25 mL) crushed red pepper

1. Mix all ingredients.

Note: Make the Chili Dressing and prep the remaining salad ingredients while the radiatore is cooking.

ORZO WITH SUN-DRIED TOMATOES AND MUSHROOMS

This simple salad is intensely flavored with sun-dried tomatoes, fresh rosemary, and sherry. If desired, the sherry can be omitted.

4 SIDE-DISH SERVINGS (ABOUT ¾ CUP [177 ML] EACH)

INGREDIENTS

2 sun-dried tomatoes, softened, sliced
1½ cups (354 mL) sliced mushrooms
¼ cup (59 mL) sliced green onions
2 cloves garlic, minced
½ cup (118 mL) canned vegetable broth
2 tablespoons (30 mL) dry sherry (optional)
½ cup (118 mL) orzo, cooked
2 tablespoons (30 mL) each: finely chopped rosemary, parsley
¼ teaspoon (1.25 mL) each: salt, pepper

1. Sauté sun-dried tomatoes, mushrooms, green onions, and garlic in lightly greased large skillet until mushrooms are tender, 5 to 7 minutes. Add broth and sherry; heat to boiling. Reduce heat and simmer, uncovered, until liquid is reduced by half, about 5 minutes; cool. Toss with orzo, herbs, salt and pepper.

FUSILLI WITH TOMATOES AND CORN >

A perfect salad, especially when homegrown tomatoes, corn, and basil are available!

8 SIDE-DISH SERVINGS

INGREDIENTS

2 cups (473 mL) chopped plum tomatoes
1 cup (236 mL) cooked whole-kernel corn
½ cup (118 mL) sliced green onions
6 ounces (170 gm) fusilli pasta (spirals), cooked, room temperature
Fresh Basil Dressing (recipe follows)

1. Combine all ingredients and toss.

FRESH BASIL DRESSING

MAKES ABOUT ⅔ CUP (158 ML)

INGREDIENTS

⅓ cup (79 mL) red wine vinegar
2 tablespoons (30 mL) olive or canola oil
3 tablespoons (45 mL) chopped fresh or 1½ teaspoons (7.5 mL) dried basil leaves
2 cloves garlic, minced
½ teaspoon (2.5 mL) salt
¼ teaspoon (1.25 mL) pepper

1. Mix all ingredients.

Note: For a shorter prep time, begin cooking the fusilli before preparing the rest of the recipe.

ASIAN NOODLE SALAD

Enjoy the wonderful blend of flavors in this salad. Thin spaghetti or linguine can be substituted for the fresh Chinese egg noodles.

4 ENTRÉE SERVINGS (ABOUT 1¼ CUPS [295 ML] EACH)

INGREDIENTS

8 ounces (224 gm) fresh Chinese egg noodles, cooked
Yogurt Dressing (recipe follows)
1 cup (236 mL) each: shredded carrot, seeded, cubed cucumber
½ cup (118 mL) chopped red bell pepper
¼ cup (59 mL) each: sliced green onions, chopped cilantro

1. Combine all ingredients and toss.

YOGURT DRESSING

MAKES ABOUT 1½ CUPS (354 ML)

INGREDIENTS

1 cup (236 mL) vegan plain yogurt
¼ cup (59 mL) reduced-fat peanut butter
2 tablespoons (30 mL) rice wine vinegar
1 tablespoon (15 mL) each: reduced-sodium tamari soy sauce, sugar, minced gingerroot
1 teaspoon (5 mL) Asian sesame oil
½ teaspoon (2.5 mL) each: 5-spice powder, minced garlic, cayenne pepper

1. Mix all ingredients.

CURRIED PASTA SALAD

This salad is especially delicious with flavored specialty pastas such as curry, lemon, sesame, or tomato.

4 ENTRÉE SERVINGS (ABOUT 1¼ CUPS [295 ML] EACH)

INGREDIENTS

⅓ cup (79 mL) chopped mango chutney
¼ cup (59 mL) chopped mixed dried fruit
2 tablespoons (30 mL) Dijon mustard
1 tablespoon (15 mL) each: olive oil, lime juice
8 ounces (224 mL) fettuccine, cooked
1 cup (236 mL) frozen stir-fry blend vegetables, cooked
Salt, cayenne pepper, and black pepper, to taste
¼ cup (59 mL) sliced green onions
2–4 tablespoons (30–60 mL) chopped cashews

1. Combine chutney, dried fruit, mustard, oil, and lime juice; spoon over fettuccine and vegetables and toss. Season to taste with salt, cayenne pepper and black pepper. Sprinkle with green onions and cashews.

GERMAN POTATO SALAD

Tart and tangy in flavor, this salad is best served warm from the skillet.

6 SIDE-DISH SERVINGS

INGREDIENTS

1 cup (236 mL) chopped onion
1 tablespoon (15 mL) flour
½ cup (118 mL) reduced-sodium canned vegetable broth
1¼ cups (295 mL) cider vinegar
1 tablespoon (15 mL) sugar
½ teaspoon (2.5 mL) celery seeds
1½ pounds (681 mL) peeled potatoes, cooked, sliced, warm
Salt and pepper, to taste
2 tablespoons (30 mL) each: crumbled cooked vegan bacon, chopped parsley

1. Sauté onion in lightly greased medium skillet until tender and browned, about 5 minutes. Stir in flour; cook 1 minute. Add broth, vinegar, sugar, and celery seeds and heat to boiling; boil, stirring, until thickened, 1 minute. Add potatoes and toss. Season to taste with salt and pepper; sprinkle with vegan bacon and parsley. Serve warm.

SPINACH AND MELON SALAD

An unusual salad, with melon adding color and flavor contrasts.

6 SIDE-DISH SERVINGS (ABOUT 1½ CUPS [354 ML) EACH)

INGREDIENTS

8 cups (1.9 L) torn spinach
1 cup (236 mL) each: watermelon, honeydew, and cantaloupe
   balls
⅓ cup (79 mL) each: thinly sliced cucumber, red onion
Spinach Salad Dressing (recipe follows)

1. Combine all ingredients and toss.

SPINACH SALAD DRESSING

MAKES ¼ CUP (59 ML)

INGREDIENTS

1–2 tablespoons (15–30 mL) maple syrup
1 tablespoon (15 mL) each: red wine vinegar, olive oil
1–2 tablespoons (15–30 mL) each: orange and lime juice
½ teaspoon (2.5 mL) dried tarragon leaves
2–3 dashes each: salt, pepper

1. Mix all ingredients.

TACO SALAD

This recipe is a bit of a production, but all your work will be rewarded with satisfied smiles from your guests. It's a great choice for brunch buffets.

8 SERVINGS

INGREDIENTS

1 pound (454 gm) dry pinto beans, soaked overnight

4 tablespoons (60 mL) canola oil, divided

1 red onion, chopped

8 cloves garlic, minced

1 tablespoon (15 mL) each: dried oregano leaves, ground cumin, dark chili powder

Salt, to taste

3 cups (708 mL) vegan chicken substitute, shredded

Freshly ground black pepper, to taste

2 heads romaine lettuce

8 tortilla shell crowns (available in Latin markets)

2 cups long-grained white rice, prepared and flavored with achiote paste, dried oregano, cumin, tumeric, and dark chili powder, to taste

2 ripe tomatoes, cut into 8 wedges each, for garnish

2 ripe avocados, sliced into 8 wedges each, for garnish

4 serrano chiles, stems removed and sliced into thin rounds, for garnish (optional)

2 cups (473 mL) store-bought pico de gallo salsa

2 cups (473 mL) Cilantro Vinaigrette (recipe follows)

1. Drain soaked pinto beans and rinse well.

2. In a large, heavy-bottomed saucepan or Dutch oven, heat 2 tablespoons (30 mL) oil over medium heat and add onion, garlic, oregano, cumin, and chili powder. Sauté until onion is soft, about 10 minutes. Add beans and water to cover them by 3 inches (7.5 cm), and stir. Heat to boiling, skimming off foam from the surface, and reduce the heat. Simmer, adding more water if necessary, until the beans are soft, about 1 hour. Season to taste with salt.

3. Heat remaining 2 tablespoons (30 mL) oil in skillet over medium heat. Add vegan chicken and sauté until browned. Season to taste with salt and pepper. Keep warm.

4. Chop lettuce. Place tortilla shell crowns on a baking sheet and warm in 350°F (180°C) oven for 3 minutes. (These tortillas will burn quite easily, so watch them carefully.)

5. To serve, place handful of lettuce at bottom of each tortilla shell crown. Follow with a few spoonfuls of Achiote Rice, a few spoonfuls of the pinto beans, and a scattering of vegan chicken. Garnish with tomato and avocado wedges and sliced serrano chiles, if desired. Serve with Pico de Gallo Salsa and Cilantro Vinaigrette.

CILANTRO VINAIGRETTE

2 SERVINGS (1 CUP [473 ML] EACH)

INGREDIENTS
1 bunch fresh cilantro, stemmed and roughly chopped
1 jalapeño pepper, seeded and roughly chopped
10 ounces (226 g) soft tofu, drained
3 tablespoons (45 mL) seasoned rice vinegar
1 cup (236 mL) canola or grapeseed oil
Juice of 1 lime
Red pepper flakes, to taste
Salt, to taste

1. In a blender or food processor, blend the cilantro, jalapeño, tofu, and rice vinegar until smooth. With the machine running, add the oil in a thin stream to form an emulsion.

2. Add the lime juice and blend again. Add red pepper flakes to taste and pulse twice.

3. Taste for seasoning and add salt as necessary.

SIDE DISHES

BOURBON STREET RED BEANS AND RICE

A New Orleans favorite, at its healthy, low-fat best!

4 ENTRÉE SERVINGS (ABOUT 1¼ CUPS [295 ML] EACH)

INGREDIENTS

1 cup (236 mL) dried red beans
2–3 cups (473–708 mL) reduced-sodium vegetable broth
1 cup (236 mL) each: chopped onion, green bell peppers, celery
½–1 jalapeño pepper, finely chopped
1 teaspoon (5 mL) each: dried thyme and oregano leaves
½ teaspoon (2.5 mL) each: dried sage leaves, ground cumin
2 bay leaves
¼ teaspoon (1.25 mL) each: red pepper sauce, cayenne pepper
4–6 drops liquid smoke
Salt, to taste
4 cups (.95 mL) cooked rice, warm

1. Cover beans with 2 inches (5 cm) water in large saucepan; heat to boiling and boil 2 minutes. Remove from heat and let stand 1 hour; drain and return to saucepan.

2. Add 2 cups (473 mL) broth to beans and heat to boiling; simmer, covered, 30 minutes. Add remaining ingredients except red pepper sauce, cayenne pepper, liquid smoke, salt and rice; simmer, covered, until beans are tender, 30 to 45 minutes, adding more broth if necessary (beans should be moist but without excess liquid). Discard bay leaves. Stir in red pepper sauce, cayenne pepper, and liquid smoke; season to taste with salt. Serve over rice.

BRAZILIAN BLACK BEAN BAKE

12 SERVINGS

INGREDIENTS

2 cups (473 mL) chopped onions

1–2 tablespoons (15–30 mL) each: minced jalapeño pepper, gingerroot

4 cans (15 ounces [425 gm] each) black beans, rinsed, drained

2 cans (14½ ounces [411 gm] each) petite-diced tomatoes, undrained

½ cup (118 mL) each: maple syrup, packed light brown sugar

¾ teaspoon (3.75 mL) each: dried thyme leaves, ground cumin

Salt and pepper, to taste

½ cup (118 mL) each: sliced mango, banana

1. Combine all ingredients, except salt, pepper, mango, and banana, in slow cooker. Cover and cook on low until beans are desired consistency, 5 to 6 hours. Season to taste with salt and pepper. Top with mango and banana before serving.

ITALIAN-STYLE BEANS AND VEGETABLES

6 SERVINGS (ABOUT 1¼ CUPS [295 ML] EACH)

INGREDIENTS

1½ cups (354 mL) each: chopped onions, Portobello mushrooms

4 cloves garlic, minced

2 tablespoons (30 mL) olive oil

2 cups (473 mL) broccoli florets and sliced stems

1 cup (236 mL) sliced yellow summer squash

1 can (15 ounces [425 gm]) each: garbanzo and red kidney beans, rinsed, drained

1 can (14½ ounces [411 gm]) reduced-sodium whole tomatoes, undrained, coarsely chopped

1 teaspoon (5 mL) dried basil leaves

½ teaspoon (2.5 mL) each: dried oregano and thyme leave

¼–½ teaspoon (1.25–2.5 mL) crushed red pepper

Salt and pepper, to taste

Polenta (recipe follows)

1. Sauté onions, mushrooms, and garlic in oil in large saucepan until tender, about 10 minutes. Add broccoli and squash; cook, covered, over medium heat 5 minutes. Stir in remaining ingredients, except salt, pepper, and Polenta; heat to boiling. Reduce heat and simmer, covered, until broccoli is tender, about 5 minutes; season to taste with salt and pepper. Serve over polenta.

POLENTA

6 SIDE-DISH SERVINGS (ABOUT ½ CUP [118 ML] EACH)

INGREDIENTS

3 cups (708 mL) water
¾ cup (177 mL) yellow cornmeal
Salt and pepper, to taste

1. Heat water to boiling; gradually stir in cornmeal. Cook over medium to medium-low heat, stirring constantly, until polenta thickens enough to hold its shape but is still soft, 5 to 8 minutes.

TUSCAN BEAN BAKE

6 SERVINGS

INGREDIENTS

3 cans (15 ounces [425 gm] each) cannellini or Great Northern beans
1 cup (236 mL) vegetable broth
½ cup (118 mL) each: chopped onion, red bell pepper
2 teaspoons (10 mL) minced garlic
1 teaspoon (5 mL) each: dried sage and rosemary leaves
2–3 teaspoons (10–15 mL) grated lemon zest
6 sun-dried tomatoes (not in oil), softened, sliced
Salt and pepper, to taste

1. Combine all ingredients, except salt and pepper, in slow cooker; cover and cook on low until beans are desired consistency, 5 to 6 hours. Season to taste with salt and pepper.

MUSTARD GREENS WITH SPINACH

This is a dish close to the hearts of most Punjabis. Everywhere you go in this rich agricultural state, you'll find bright green fields with yellow flowers where mustard greens have been planted. Bollywood actors dance through these fields in love scenes and sing about them longingly. This recipe comes from The Indian Slow Cooker *by Anupy Singla.*

10 SERVINGS (1 CUP EACH)

INGREDIENTS

1 pound (454 gm) mustard greens, trimmed and washed thoroughly
1 pound (454 gm) spinach, trimmed and washed thoroughly
1 large yellow or red onion, roughly chopped
1 (2-inch [(5 cm]) piece gingerroot, chopped
15 cloves garlic
6–8 green Thai or Serrano chiles, or cayenne peppers, stems removed
1 tablespoon (15 mL) ground coriander
2 tablespoons (30 mL) cornmeal
1½ tablespoons (22.5 mL) salt
1 teaspoon (5 mL) turmeric powder
2 cups (473 mL) water
1 teaspoon (5 mL) garam masala

1. Combine mustard greens, spinach, onion, gingerroot, garlic, green chiles, coriander, cornmeal, salt, turmeric, and water in slow cooker; cover and cook on high 6 hours.

2. Using an immersion blender, blend until smooth, or transfer to blender and process, returning mixture to slow cooker. Add garam masala. Cook in a slow cooker on low 1 hour. Serve with Indian breads, such as corn rotis, regular rotis, or naan.

To make this dish in a 3½-quart slow cooker, halve all the ingredients and proceed with the recipe. A half recipe makes 5 cups (1.18 L).

GREEK-STYLE GREEN BEANS

8–10 SERVINGS

INGREDIENTS

1 pound (454 gm) green beans
1 can (28 ounces [794 gm]) petite-diced tomatoes, undrained
½ cup (118 mL) chopped onion
4 cloves garlic, minced
¾ teaspoon (3.75 mL) each: dried oregano and basil leaves
Salt and pepper, to taste

1. Combine all ingredients, except salt and pepper, in slow cooker; cover and cook on high until beans are tender, about 4 hours. Season to taste with salt and pepper.

ORANGE CILANTRO RICE >

6 SIDE-DISH SERVINGS

INGREDIENTS

½ cup (118 mL) sliced green onions
1 cup (236 mL) uncooked long-grain rice
Grated zest of 1 small orange
2¼ cups (531 mL) water
2 tablespoons (30 mL) finely chopped cilantro
Salt and pepper, to taste

1. Sauté onions in lightly greased medium saucepan until tender, 3 to 5 minutes. Add rice and orange zest; stir over medium heat until rice is lightly browned, 2 to 3 minutes. Add water and heat to boiling; reduce heat and simmer, covered, until rice is tender, 20 to 25 minutes. Stir in cilantro; season to taste with salt and pepper.

BRAISED WHOLE ARTICHOKES

4 SERVINGS

INGREDIENTS

4 medium artichokes, stems removed
Salt
2–4 teaspoons (10–20 mL) olive oil

1. Cut 1 inch (2.5 cm) from tops of artichokes and discard. Place artichokes in medium saucepan and sprinkle lightly with salt; add 1 inch (2.5 cm) water to pan. Heat to boiling; reduce heat and simmer, covered, until artichokes are tender, about 30 minutes (bottom leaves will pull out easily).

2. Drain. Holding artichokes with a towel, brush bottoms with olive oil; return to saucepan. Cook, uncovered, over medium to medium-low heat until bottoms of artichokes are deeply browned, 10 to 15 minutes.

EGGPLANT AND VEGETABLE SAUTÉ

Minced roasted garlic is available in jars in your produce section; substitute fresh minced garlic if desired.

6 SERVINGS

INGREDIENTS

1 large eggplant (about 1¼ pounds [567 gm]), unpeeled, cubed

1½ cups (354 mL) each: sliced red or green bell peppers, onions

4 teaspoons (20 mL) minced roasted garlic

½ teaspoon (2.5 mL) each: dried rosemary and thyme leaves

2 teaspoons (10 mL) olive oil

1 can (15 ounces [425 gm]) cannellini or Great Northern beans, rinsed, drained

Salt and pepper, to taste

1. Cook eggplant, bell pepper, onions, garlic, rosemary, and thyme in oil in large saucepan over medium heat, covered, until vegetables are tender, 8 to 10 minutes; stir in beans and cook until hot, about 2 minutes. Season to taste with salt and pepper.

BROCCOLI RABE SAUTÉED WITH GARLIC

This simple flavorful vegetable recipe can also be made with broccoli, green beans, or asparagus.

4–6 SERVINGS

INGREDIENTS

1 pound (454 gm) broccoli rabe, cooked crisp-tender
4 cloves garlic, minced
Salt and pepper, to taste

1. Sauté broccoli rabe and garlic in lightly greased large skillet until broccoli rabe begins to brown, 4 to 5 minutes. Season to taste with salt and pepper.

CURRIED SWEET POTATO COUSCOUS

Versatile couscous blends easily with a variety of vegetable flavors.

4 ENTRÉE SERVINGS

INGREDIENTS

¼ cup (59 mL) sliced onion
2 cloves garlic, minced
1–2 tablespoons (15–30 mL) olive oil
2 medium sweet potatoes, peeled, cooked, diced
1–1½ teaspoons (5–7.5 mL) curry powder
¼ cup (59 mL) each: raisins, walnuts
1 cup (236 mL) reduced-sodium vegetable broth
⅔ cup (158 mL) couscous
1 cup (236 mL) thinly sliced kale
Salt and pepper, to taste

1. Sauté onion and garlic in olive oil in large saucepan until tender, 2 to 3 minutes. Add sweet potatoes; cook until lightly browned, about 5 minutes. Stir in curry powder, raisins, walnuts, and broth; heat to boiling. Add couscous and kale, stirring with a fork; remove from heat and let stand, covered, until couscous is tender and broth is absorbed, about 5 minutes. Season to taste with salt and pepper.

ASIAN PILAF

A combination of brown rice, millet, and Asian ingredients make this pilaf a favorite.

4 ENTRÉE SERVINGS

INGREDIENTS

⅓ cup (79 ml) each: chopped onion, celery
2–3 teaspoons (10–15 mL) finely chopped gingerroot, garlic
1 tablespoon (15 mL) Asian sesame oil
½ cup (118 mL) each: brown rice, millet
2½ cups (591 mL) reduced-sodium vegetable broth
1½ cups (354 mL) halved snow peas
½ can (6-ounce size [170-gm]) water chestnuts, drained, sliced
½ cup (59 mL) thinly sliced green onions
2–3 tablespoons (30–45 mL) reduced-sodium tamari soy sauce
Salt and pepper, to taste

1. Sauté onion, celery, gingerroot, and garlic in sesame oil in large saucepan until onion is tender, about 10 minutes. Add rice and millet and cook 2 minutes longer; add broth and heat to boiling. Reduce heat and simmer, covered, 15 minutes. Stir in snow peas, water chestnuts, and green onions; simmer, covered, until grains and snow peas are tender and broth absorbed, about 10 minutes. Season to taste with soy sauce, salt, and pepper.

MUSHROOM AND ASPARAGUS PILAF

The dried Chinese black or shiitake mushrooms impart a hearty, woodsy flavor to this pilaf.

8 ENTRÉE SERVINGS (ABOUT 1½ CUPS [354 ML] EACH)

INGREDIENTS

3⅓ cups (787 mL) reduced-sodium vegetable broth, divided
2 cups (473 mL) dried Chinese mushrooms
2 cups (473 mL) chopped onions
4 cloves garlic, minced
2 teaspoons (10 mL) dried basil leaves
½ teaspoon (2.5 mL) each: dried thyme and savory leaves
1½ pounds (680 mL) asparagus, cut into 1½-inch (3.5-cm) pieces
¼ cup (59 mL) dry sherry, or water
2 packages (6 ounces [170 gm] each) tabbouleh wheat salad mix (spice packet discarded)
¼ teaspoon (1.25 mL) red pepper sauce
Salt and pepper, to taste
4 green onions, thinly sliced
¼ cup (59 mL) toasted pecan halves

1. Heat 2 cups (473 mL) broth to boiling; pour over mushrooms in bowl and let stand until mushrooms are softened, 10 to 15 minutes. Drain; reserve broth. Slice mushrooms, discarding tough stems.

2. Sauté mushrooms, onions, garlic, basil, thyme, and savory in lightly greased large skillet until onions are tender, about 5 minutes. Add asparagus, sherry, reserved mushroom broth, and remaining 1⅓ cups (314 mL) broth; heat to boiling. Stir in tabbouleh; reduce heat and simmer, covered, until tabbouleh is tender and broth absorbed, 3 to 5 minutes. Stir in red pepper sauce; season to taste with salt and pepper. Sprinkle with green onions and pecans.

QUINOA WITH ROASTED EGGPLANT AND SQUASH

Grain recipes are versatile, as almost any grain can be used in them. Couscous, millet, or kasha also would be excellent choices in this recipe.

4 ENTRÉE SERVINGS (ABOUT 1½ CUPS [354 ML] EACH)

INGREDIENTS

1 small butternut squash, peeled, cubed
1 medium unpeeled eggplant, cubed
1 cup (236 mL) each: thickly sliced bell pepper, onion
Vegetable oil cooking spray
1 teaspoon (5 mL) dried rosemary leaves
½ teaspoon (2.5 mL) each: dried savory and thyme leaves
2 cups (354 mL) reduced-sodium vegetable broth
1 cup (236 mL) quinoa
Salt and pepper, to taste

1. Arrange vegetables in single layer on greased foil-lined jelly-roll pan. Spray vegetables with cooking spray; sprinkle with rosemary, davory, and thyme. Roast at 425°F (220°C) until vegetables are tender, 35 to 45 minutes.

2. Heat broth to boiling in medium saucepan; stir in quinoa. Reduce heat and simmer, covered, until quinoa is tender and broth absorbed, about 15 minutes. Combine quinoa and warm vegetables; season to taste with salt and pepper.

MEXI-BEANS, GREENS, AND RICE

Hotly spiced, the chilies and cayenne pepper in this dish can be decreased if less hotness is desired. Four cans (15 ounces each) pinto beans, rinsed and drained, can be substituted for the dried beans; delete step 1 in recipe.

8 MAIN-DISH SERVINGS (ABOUT 1¼ CUPS EACH)

INGREDIENTS

2 cups dried pinto beans
1 each: chopped onion, poblano chili, red bell pepper
4 cloves garlic, minced
1 tablespoon each: finely chopped gingerroot, serrano chilies
2 tablespoons olive oil
2 cups reduced-sodium vegetable broth, or water
2–3 teaspoons chili powder
2 teaspoons dried oregano leaves
1 teaspoon ground cumin
¼ teaspoon cayenne pepper
1 can (15 ounces) diced tomatoes, undrained
2 cups coarsely chopped turnip, or mustard, greens
Salt, to taste
5 cups cooked rice, warm
Cilantro, finely chopped, as garnish

1. Cover beans with 2 inches water in large saucepan; heat to boiling and boil, uncovered, 2 minutes. Remove from heat and let stand, covered, 1 hour; drain.

2. Sauté onion, poblano chili, bell pepper, garlic, gingerroot, and serrano chilies in oil in large saucepan until tender, 8 to 10 minutes. Add beans, broth and seasonings; heat to boiling. Reduce heat and simmer, covered, until beans are tender, 1 to 1¼ hours, adding water if necessary. Stir in tomatoes and greens; simmer, uncovered, to desired thickness, 15 to 30 minutes. Season to taste with salt. Serve over rice; sprinkle generously with cilantro.

ORANGE-GLAZED BABY CARROTS

        1 pound (454 gm) baby carrots
        ¾ cup (177 mL) orange juice
        1 tablespoon (15 mL) vegan margarine
        ½ cup (118 mL) packed light brown sugar
        ½ teaspoon (2.5 mL) ground cinnamon
        ¼ teaspoon (1.25 mL) ground mace
        2 tablespoons (30 mL) cornstarch
        ¼ cup (59 mL) water
        Salt and white pepper, to taste

1. Combine all ingredients, except cornstarch, water, salt, and white pepper, in slow cooker; cover and cook on high until carrots are crisp-tender, about 3 hours. Keep heat on high and cook 10 minutes. Stir in combined cornstarch and water, stirring 2 to 3 minutes; season to taste with salt and pepper.

SUGAR-GLAZED BRUSSELS SPROUTS AND PEARL ONIONS >

Large Brussels sprouts can be halved for faster cooking. The pearl onions can be fresh, frozen, or canned.

4–6 SERVINGS

INGREDIENTS

1 tablespoon (15 mL) vegan margarine
¼ cup (59 mL) sugar
8 ounces (224 mL) each: small Brussels sprouts, pearl onions, cooked until crisp-tender, warm
Salt and white pepper, to taste

1. Heat margarine in medium skillet until melted; stir in sugar and cook over medium heat until mixture is bubbly. Add vegetables and toss to coat. Season to taste with salt and white pepper.

CHUNKY APPLESAUCE

Great served warm, or chilled, as an accompaniment to entrées.

6 SERVINGS

INGREDIENTS

3 pounds (1.4 kg) Jonathan apples, peeled, coarsely chopped
⅔ cup (158 mL) water
½ cup (118 mL) sugar
Ground cinnamon

1. Combine all ingredients, except cinnamon, in slow cooker; cover and cook on high until apples are very soft, and form applesauce when stirred, 2 to 2½ hours. Sprinkle with cinnamon when serving.

DESSERTS

APPLE-CRANBERRY CRISP

Apples and cranberries are happy companions in this streusel-topped fruit crisp.

6 SERVINGS

INGREDIENTS

2½ pounds (1.2 kg) cooking apples, peeled, cored, sliced
1 cup (236 mL) fresh, or frozen, thawed cranberries
½ cup (118 mL) packed light brown sugar
2 tablespoons (30 mL) all-purpose flour
1 teaspoon (5 mL) finely chopped crystallized ginger
Streusel Topping (recipe follows)

1. Combine all ingredients, except Streusel Topping, in 1-quart (.95 L) glass casserole; sprinkle with Streusel Topping. Bake, uncovered, at 350°F (180°C) until apples are tender, 30 to 40 minutes. Serve warm.

STREUSEL TOPPING

INGREDIENTS

⅓ cup (79 mL) quick-cooking oats
3 tablespoons (45 mL) each: all-purpose flour, packed light brown sugar
1½ tablespoons (22.5 mL) cold vegan margarine

1. Combine oats, flour, and brown sugar in small bowl; cut in vegan margarine until mixture resembles coarse crumbs.

OATMEAL–CHOCOLATE CHIP COOKIES

24 SERVINGS (1 COOKIE EACH)

INGREDIENTS

2 cups (473 mL) unbleached all-purpose flour
1 teaspoon (5 mL) ground cinnamon
1 teaspoon (5 mL) baking soda
½ teaspoon (2.5 mL) salt
½ cup vegan shortening
1 cup (236 mL) sugar
½ cup (118 mL) unsweetened applesauce
⅓ cup (79 mL) molasses
2 cups (473 mL) quick-cooking or old-fashioned oats
1 cup (236 mL) vegan mini chocolate chips

1. Preheat oven to 400°F (200°C). Combine the flour, cinnamon, baking soda, and salt with wire whisk and set aside.

2. In bowl of a stand mixer fitted with paddle attachment, beat shortening, sugar, applesauce, and molasses until smooth. Add flour mixture and beat well.

3. Line baking sheet with parchment paper. Stir oats and raisins into cookie dough. Using a cookie scooper, place dough onto prepared baking sheet. Bake 7 to 10 minutes, or until lightly browned. Remove from the oven, press down slightly on cookies, and let cool completely on baking sheet.

FARMER'S MARKET CHERRY CAKE

This is delicious plain or sprinkled with confectioners' sugar and served with a dollop of soy ice cream. It is best when you can use fabulous fresh cherries from your local farmer's market in the summer. This recipe comes from Vegan Baking Classics *by Kelly Rudnicki.*

10 SERVINGS

INGREDIENTS

1½ cups (354 mL) unbleached all-purpose flour
1½ teaspoons (7.5 mL) baking powder
⅛ teaspoon (.7 mL) salt
½ cup (118 mL) silken tofu
¾ cup (177 mL) sugar
½ cup (118 mL) vegan margarine, melted, cooled to room temperature
⅓ cup (79 mL) soy or rice milk
1 teaspoon (5 mL) vanilla extract
2 teaspoons (10 mL) grated lemon zest
1 tablespoon (15 mL) lemon juice
1 pint fresh cherries, pitted

1. Preheat oven to 400°F (200°C). Combine the flour, baking powder, and salt with wire whisk, and set aside.

2. In bowl of a stand mixer fitted with paddle attachment, beat tofu and sugar on medium-high speed until light and fluffy, about 2 minutes. Add margarine, soy milk, vanilla, lemon zest, and lemon juice, and mix well. Add flour mixture, stirring until just combined. Lightly fold in cherries.

3. Spray 9-inch springform pan with vegan baking spray. Transfer batter to prepared pan. Bake cake for 30 to 35 minutes, or until light golden brown and an inserted cake tester comes out clean. Cool completely on wire rack.

PEANUT BUTTER COOKIES

INGREDIENTS

3 cups (708 mL) unbleached white spelt flour
1½ teaspoons (7.5 mL) baking powder
½ teaspoon (2.5 mL) baking soda
1 teaspoon (5 mL) salt
1 teaspoon (5 mL) ground cinnamon or allspice
1 cup (236 mL) creamy peanut butter
½ cup (118 mL) vegan margarine, softened
¼ cup (59 mL) maple or agave syrup
1 tablespoon (15 mL) arrowroot powder
2 teaspoons (10 mL) pure vanilla extract
2 tablespoons (30 mL) warm water

1. Preheat the oven to 350°F (180°C). Line two baking sheets with parchment paper and lightly oil paper.

2. Combine flour, baking powder, baking soda, salt, and cinnamon with wire whisk.

3. In separate bowl, combine peanut butter, margarine, maple, arrowroot, vanilla, and warm water. Stir until creamy and smooth.

4. Using a hand mixer, slowly blend dry ingredients into wet ingredients. If dough does not come together properly add a little canola or safflower oil. (You may need to work the dough together with your hands.)

5. Drop scoopfuls of cookie dough onto prepared sheets. Press dough with fork in criss-cross pattern.

6. Bake 15 to 18 minutes. Remove from the oven and let cool for 30 minutes before removing from sheets and transferring them to cooling rack.

LEMON CAKE

12 SERVINGS

LEMON CAKE INGREDIENTS

2½ cups (591 mL) unbleached all-purpose flour
½ teaspoon (2.5 mL) baking soda
¼ teaspoon (1.25 mL) salt
½ cup (118 mL) vegan margarine
1½ cups (354 mL) granulated sugar
¾ cup (177 mL) silken tofu
1 teaspoon (5 mL) grated lemon zest
½ cup (118 mL) soy or rice milk
¼ cup (59 mL) freshly squeezed lemon juice

CREAMY GLAZE INGREDIENTS

2 cups (473 mL) confectioners' sugar
1 teaspoon (5 mL) grated lemon zest
½ teaspoon (2.5 mL) vanilla extract
3–4 teaspoons (15–20 mL) soy or rice milk

1. Preheat oven to 350°F (180°C), and spray 13 × 9-inch (33 × 23-cm) baking dish with vegan baking spray. Set aside.

2. Combine flour, baking soda, and salt with wire whisk and set aside.

3. In bowl of a stand mixer fitted with paddle attachment, beat margarine and granulated sugar until light and fluffy. Add tofu and 1 teaspoon lemon zest, and beat well. Add flour mixture, alternating additions with soy milk, and beat well. Stir in lemon juice.

4. Transfer the batter to the prepared baking dish, and bake 25 to 30 minutes, or until an inserted cake tester comes out clean. Cool completely on wire rack.

5. Combine Creamy Glaze ingredients in small bowl, and drizzle glaze over cooled cake.

PUMPKIN COOKIES

These are little buttons of pumpkin with a creamy glaze spread on top. They are a perfect pumpkin treat.

24 SERVINGS (1 COOKIE EACH)

INGREDIENTS

3 cups (708 mL) unbleached all-purpose flour
1 tablespoon (15 mL) baking powder
1 teaspoon (5 mL) ground cinnamon
¼ teaspoon (1.25 mL) ground nutmeg
¼ teaspoon (1.25 mL) ground ginger
¼ teaspoon (1.25 mL) salt
½ cup (118 mL) vegan shortening
1½ cups (354 mL) packed light brown sugar
½ cup (118 mL) unsweetened applesauce
1 (15-ounce [425 gm]) can pumpkin purée (not pumpkin pie filling)
Classic Icing (recipe follows)

1. Preheat oven to 400°F (200°F). Line 2 baking sheets with parchment paper. Set aside.

2. Combine flour, baking powder, cinnamon, nutmeg, ginger, and salt with wire whisk.

3. In bowl of a stand mixer fitted with paddle attachment, beat shortening, brown sugar, applesauce, and pumpkin until well mixed. Add flour mixture, and stir until just combined.

4. Using a cookie scooper, place dough on prepared baking sheets. Bake 12 to 15 minutes, or until lightly browned. Cool on wire rack. Frost cookies with Classic Icing.

CLASSIC ICING

INGREDIENTS

2 cups (473 mL) confectioners' sugar

1 teaspoon (5 mL) vanilla extract

3–4 tablespoons (45–60 mL) soy or rice milk, as needed to thin icing

1. Blend all ingredients together in small bowl with wire whisk. Drizzle over Pumpkin Cookies, or dip each cookie into icing.

CLASSIC CHOCOLATE BIRTHDAY CUPCAKES

This recipe's batter can be used to make an 8-inch layer cake, a 13 × 9-inch rectangular cake, or 24 cupcakes. This recipe comes from Vegan Baking Classics *by Kelly Rudnicki.*

24 SERVINGS (1 CUPCAKE EACH)

INGREDIENTS

2 cups (473 mL) cake flour
1½ cups (354 mL) sugar
⅔ cup (158 mL) cocoa powder
1½ teaspoons (7.5 mL) baking soda
½ teaspoon (2.5 mL) salt
½ cup (118 mL) vegan shortening
1½ cups (354 mL) vegan buttermilk (or 1½ cups [354 mL] soy or rice milk mixed with 1½ tablespoons [22.5 mL] white vinegar; let stand for 5–10 minutes)
2 tablespoons (30 mL) water
1 teaspoon (5 mL) vanilla extract
Classic Icing (see page 141)

1. Preheat oven to 350°F (180°C). Line 24 cupcake cups with paper liners. Set aside.

2. Combine cake flour, sugar, cocoa powder, baking soda, and salt with wire whisk.

3. In bowl of a stand mixer fitted with paddle attachment, beat shortening, buttermilk, water, and vanilla until well mixed. Slowly add flour mixture to the shortening mixture, and beat on high 3 to 4 minutes.

4. Pour batter evenly into liners, and bake 20 to 25 minutes. Cool completely before frosting.

GINGER-CITRUS SORBET

Slightly tart, slightly zesty, very refreshing!

6 SERVINGS

INGREDIENTS

3½ cups (826 mL) water
1½ cups (354 mL) sugar
¼ cup (59 mL) minced gingerroot
2 teaspoons (10 mL) finely grated orange zest
⅓ cup (79 mL) orange juice
2 tablespoons (30 mL) lemon juice

1. Heat water, sugar, gingerroot, and orange zest to boiling in medium saucepan, stirring until sugar is dissolved. Reduce heat and simmer 7 to 10 minutes; cool. Stir in orange and lemon juices.

2. Freeze mixture in ice cream maker according to manufacturer's directions. Or pour into 8-inch-square (20-cm-square) baking pan and freeze until slushy, 2 to 4 hours; spoon into bowl and beat until fluffy, then return to pan and freeze until firm, 6 hours.

SUMMER BLUEBERRY PIE >

6 SERVINGS

EASY PIE DOUGH INGREDIENTS

2 cups (473 mL) unbleached all-purpose flour
1 teaspoon (5 mL) sugar
½ teaspoon (2.5 mL) salt
⅔ cup (158 mL) vegan shortening, cold, cut into small pieces
5–7 tablespoons (75–105 mL) ice water

FILLING INGREDIENTS

6 cups (1.4 L) fresh blueberries
¾ cup (177 mL) sugar
3 tablespoons (45 mL) unbleached all-purpose flour
¾ teaspoon (3.75 mL) grated lemon zest
1 teaspoon (5 mL) fresh lemon juice
½ teaspoon (2.5 mL) ground cinnamon
⅛ teaspoon (.7 mL) salt
1 tablespoon (15 mL) vegan margarine
Sugar, for sprinkling

1. Combine 2 cups (473 mL) flour, 1 teaspoon (5 mL) sugar, and ½ teaspoon (2.5 mL) salt in bowl of food processor. Add shortening, and pulse a few times until the mixture resembles small crumbs. Add ice water slowly, pulsing until the dough just comes together. Transfer dough to sheet of plastic wrap. Use plastic wrap to pull edge of dough together, forming a disk. Chill at least 30 minutes before using.

2. In large bowl, combine blueberries, ¾ cup (177 mL) sugar, 3 tablespoons (45 mL) flour, lemon zest, lemon juice, cinnamon, and ⅛ teaspoon (.7 mL) salt, mixing well.

3. Preheat oven to 400°F (200°C). Divide dough in half. On floured surface, roll out each half into 12-inch circle. Line bottom of 9-inch (23-cm) pie plate with half of dough. Pour blueberry mixture into pie shell and dot mixture with margarine. Cover blueberries with remaining half of dough, crimping edges together with your fingers. Cut four 1-inch slits in top crust, and sprinkle pie with sugar.

4. Bake about 45 minutes, or until filling is bubbling and crust is golden brown. Remove from oven, and cool completely on wire rack.

LEMON ICE

Serve this sweet-and-tart ice as a dessert or as a refreshing palate cleanser between dinner courses.

8 SERVINGS

INGREDIENTS
2 cups (473 mL) water
½ cup (118 mL) grated lemon zest
1 cup (236 mL) each: sugar, lemon juice

1. Heat water, sugar, lemon zest, and lemon juice to boiling in medium saucepan, stirring until sugar is dissolved. Reduce heat and simmer, uncovered, 5 minutes; cool.

2. Freeze mixture in ice cream maker according to manufacturer's directions, or pour into 8-inch-square (20-cm-square) baking pan and freeze until slushy, about 2 hours. Spoon into bowl and beat until fluffy, then return to pan and freeze until firm, 6 hours or overnight.

DOUBLE EVIL BROWNIES

12 SERVINGS

INGREDIENTS
3 cups (708 mL) unbleached white spelt flour
1½ teaspoons (7.5 mL) baking powder
½ teaspoon (2.5 mL) baking soda
1 teaspoon (5 mL) salt
¾ cup (177 mL) unsweetened cocoa powder
10 ounces (284 gm) firm tofu, broken into chunks
1¾ cups (413 mL) turbinado sugar
¾ cup (177 mL) canola oil
1 cup (236 mL) rice or soy milk
1 tablespoon (15 mL) vanilla extract
2 tablespoons (30 mL) water
⅔ cup (158 mL) vegan chocolate chips (optional)
⅔ cup (158 mL) chopped walnuts (optional)
⅔ cup (158 mL) shredded coconut (optional)
Confectioners' sugar, for dusting (optional)

1. Preheat oven to 350°F (180°C). Line 13 × 9-inch (33 × 23-cm) baking pan with parchment paper and oil paper and sides of pan.

2. Combine flour, baking powder, baking soda, salt, and cocoa powder with wire whisk.

3. In separate bowl, combine tofu, turbinado sugar, oil, rice milk, vanilla, and water and mix well.

4. Slowly add tofu mixture to flour mixture, blending with hand mixer until smooth. Stir in optional ingredients, if desired. Pour mixture into prepared baking pan. If you like, decorate the top with additional chocolate chips or nuts.

5. Bake about 25 minutes or until an inserted cake tester comes out dry. Cool on wire rack.

6. Dust with confectioners' sugar before serving, if desired.

INDEX

ABOUT THE SERIES

Each of the books in the *101* series feature delicious, diverse, and accessible recipes—101 of them, to be exact. Scattered throughout each book are beautiful full-color photographs to show you just what the dish should look like. The *101* series books also feature a simple, contemporary design that's as practical as it is elegant, with measures calculated in both traditional and metric quantities.

ABOUT THE EDITOR

Kate DeVivo is co-editor of Surrey's *101* series. She lives with her family in Chicago.

Also from Agate Surrey

The Indian Slow Cooker
50 HEALTHY, EASY, AUTHENTIC RECIPES | Anupy Singla

"Singla's book goes against what many believe is required of Indian cuisine—infusing hot oil with a whole mess of spices as the base for dishes. Instead, she argues, throw everything into the Crock-Pot and let the aromatics do their thing ... the book gives old- and new-school cooks alike ample reason to give Indian food a shot."

Janet Rausa Fuller, *Chicago Sun-Times*

ISBN 978-157284-11-16 · $19.95

Available at booksellers everywhere

SURREY
BOOKS

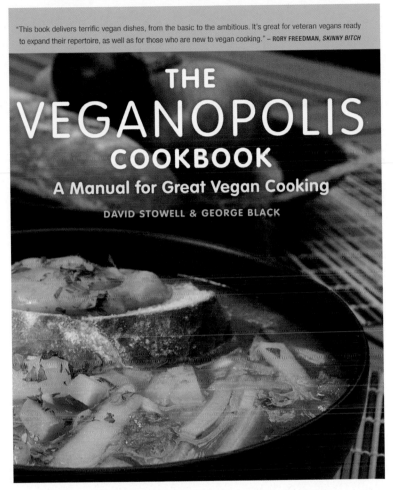